ENVISIONING HEIJŌKYŌ

100 QUESTIONS & ANSWERS ABOUT THE ANCIENT CAPITAL IN NARA, JAPAN

I0428592

TRANSLATED AND ADAPTED BY

YOKO HSUEH SHIRAI

BASED ON THE ORIGINAL JAPANESE EDITION
BY ARCHAEOLOGICAL INSTITUTE OF KASHIHARA,
NARA PREFECTURE

Originally published in 2010, in Japanese, under the title
Heijōkyō 100 no gimon by Gakuseisha Ltd., Tokyo.

Copyright © 2011 Yoko Hsueh SHIRAI
All rights reserved.

ISBN: 1463768222

ISBN 13: 9781463768225

Library of Congress Control Number: 2011913478
CreateSpace, North Charleston, SC

CONTENTS

LIST OF ILLUSTRATIONS

MAPS

(courtesy of Archaeological Institute of Kashihara, Nara Prefecture)

FIGURES

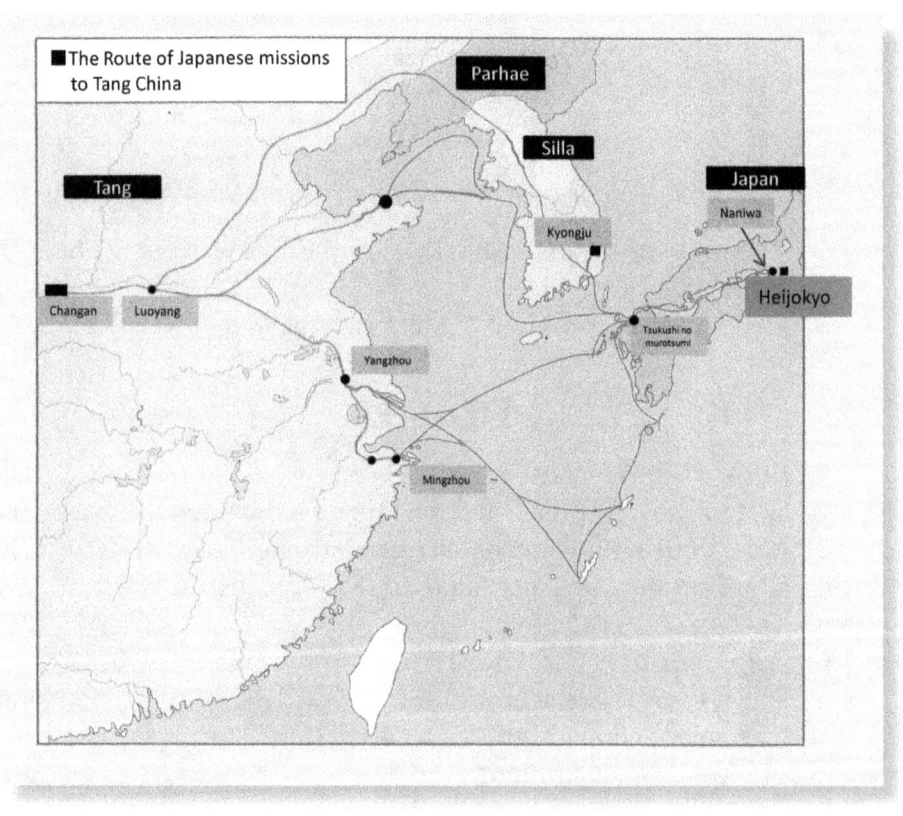

Map 1.

The route of Japanese missions from Heijōkyō to Tang China

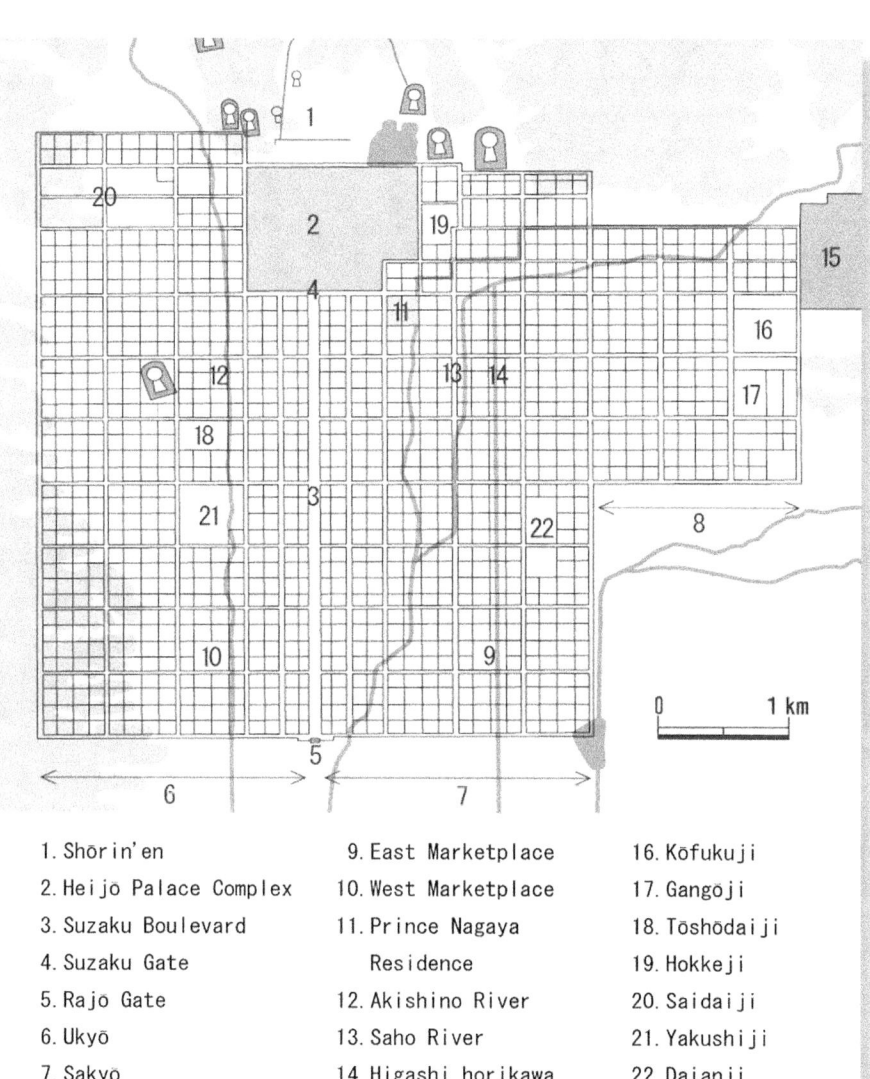

1. Shōrin'en
2. Heijō Palace Complex
3. Suzaku Boulevard
4. Suzaku Gate
5. Rajō Gate
6. Ukyō
7. Sakyō
8. Gekyō
9. East Marketplace
10. West Marketplace
11. Prince Nagaya Residence
12. Akishino River
13. Saho River
14. Higashi horikawa
15. Tōdaiji
16. Kōfukuji
17. Gangōji
18. Tōshōdaiji
19. Hokkeji
20. Saidaiji
21. Yakushiji
22. Daianji

Map 2.
Heijōkyō

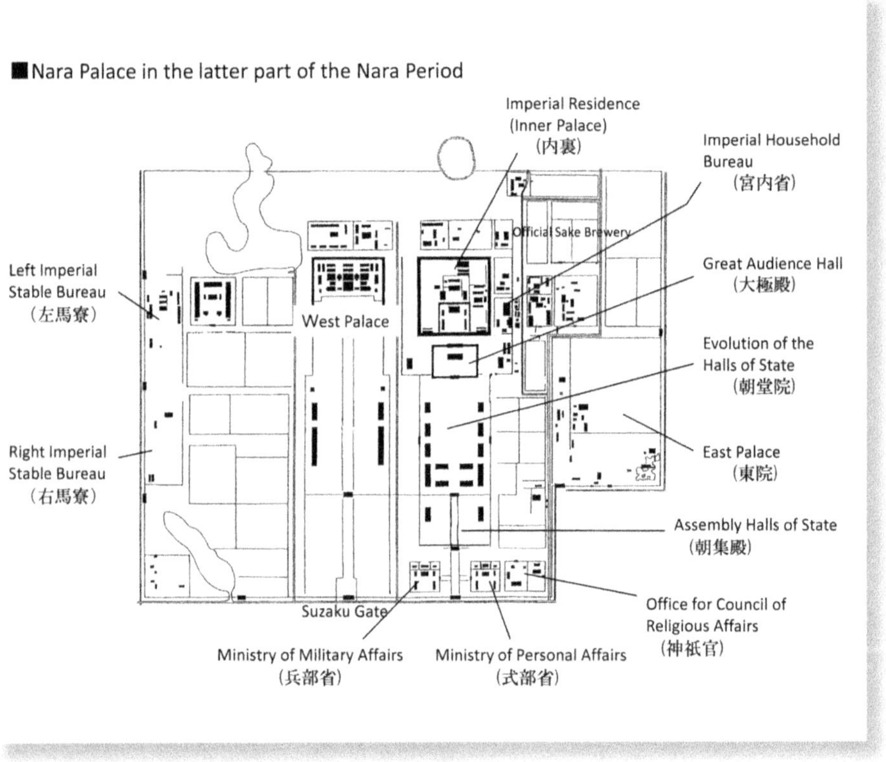

■Nara Palace in the latter part of the Nara Period

Imperial Residence
(Inner Palace)
(内裏)

Imperial Household
Bureau
(宮内省)

Left Imperial
Stable Bureau
(左馬寮)

West Palace

Official Sake Brewery

Great Audience Hall
(大極殿)

Evolution of the
Halls of State
(朝堂院)

Right Imperial
Stable Bureau
(右馬寮)

East Palace
(東院)

Assembly Halls of State
(朝集殿)

Office for Council of
Religious Affairs
(神祇官)

Suzaku Gate

Ministry of Military Affairs
(兵部省)

Ministry of Personal Affairs
(式部省)

Map 3.
Heijō palace complex in the late Nara period

Figure 1.
Suzaku Gate (reconstructed)

Figure 2.
Distant view of Great Audience Hall (reconstructed)

Figure 3.
View of Great Audience Hall (reconstructed) with diagram

Figure 4.
Close-up view of Great Audience Hall (reconstructed)

Figure 5.
Tōin teien (reconstructed garden)

Figure 6.
Ship (reconstructed) used to transport envoys across the seas

Figure 7.
The palace complex gift shop during the 1300ᵗʰ anniversary celebrations

Figure 8.

Sentokun: official mascot of the 1300th anniversary of Heijōkyō

TRANSLATOR'S NOTE

Ever since I conducted field work on early Buddhist statuary at the Archaeological Institute of Kashihara, Nara Prefecture (Nara kenritsu Kashihara kōkogaku kenkyūjo) as a Japan Foundation doctoral fellow, I often returned to visit this active center of excavation and research. During my last visit in February 2011 the general director, Sugaya Fuminori, asked me to translate the Japanese edition of this book into English.

Envisioning Heijōkyō draws upon years of painstaking archaeological survey to provide readers an easily accessible, detailed introduction to the eighth-century capital at Nara. Exciting discoveries have revealed striking contrasts between the everyday lives of commoners and the glittering lifestyles of Heijōkyō's aristocratic elite. One characteristic distinguishing this book from many others in the same genre is an attempt to portray the broad spectrum of life at one of the earliest, planned capitals in Japan. Styles of homes and buildings, family structures, diets, taxes, modes of entertainment, prayer, and even pets are included in this broad, eclectic survey.

While *Envisioning Heijōkyō* is a translation of the original Japanese edition, it is also an adaptation. Most notably, I inserted footnotes and a glossary to assist readers' understanding of Japanese words and concepts. As translator, I tried to replicate the same conversational tone of voice that appears in the Japanese edition.

With regard to images, an online version of the Japanese edition is available at http://www.kashikoken.jp/news/2009/rist.html, and color reproductions usually accompany each question-and-answer link. While the sequence of questions in the online version and the book do not match exactly, all questions do appear in both versions. The English edition also includes some of my own photos, taken during a 2010 visit to Nara during the 1300th anniversary celebrations of the Heijō capital. As for the three maps, I am grateful to the Archaeological Institute of Kashihara, Nara Prefecture, for graciously providing these reproductions.

If you plan to visit the expansive Heijō palace grounds, prepare to spend several hours walking among the reconstructed buildings, wandering the gardens, and observing the artifacts displayed at the on-site museum of the Nara National Research Institute for Cultural Properties. *Envisioning Heijōkyō* is one of the first books of its kind to appear in English. I hope you will enjoy reading the book as much as I did.

Preface to the Japanese Edition

In the third month of the third year of Wadō (710 CE), Heavenly Sovereign Genmei (Genmei tennō) relocated her court from the Fujiwara palace complex (Fujiwarakyū) to the Heijō palace complex (Heijōkyū) in what is today Nara city. This event is referred to as the Heijō sento, or the transfer of the capital to Heijō. Exactly thirteen hundred years have elapsed between the year of the transfer and 2010.

During this long span of time, the Heijō palace complex has fallen into ruin and much of the surrounding capital (Heijōkyō) has reverted to rice fields. Traces of the ancient capital largely disappeared; for instance, the site once occupied by an important building formerly used by Heavenly Sovereigns, Great Audience Hall (Daigokuden), still retained the name "Daikoku no shiba" but only an earthen platform remained extant at the site.[1]

After a long period of obscurity, the spotlight returned to Heijōkyō at some point between the end of the Edo period and the early Meiji period.[2] A government official named Kitaura Sadamasa, from the Tōdō feudal domain in what is now Mie prefecture, investigated the history of local place names at the site, in addition to taking measurements of the banks of rice fields in an attempt to locate past building activity. Kitaura subsequently became the first person to clearly identify and

---

[1] Although the two terms sound similar, the Chinese characters for *daigoku* and *daikoku* differ. *Shiba* translates to "grass." Presumably the local inhabitants continued to call this site *daigoku* or *daikoku*, but over time the correct transcription was lost.

[2] The feudal, premodern Edo period lasted from 1603 to 1867/1868, and the end of Edo generally refers to 1853-1869. The Meiji period extended from 1868 through 1912.

indicate traces of the Heijō capital. Aside from Kitaura, an architectural historian named Sekino Tadashi (1868-1935) conducted detailed surveys and proposed reconstructed models of the Heijō palace complex and capital. Scholarly contributions made by Kitaura and Sekino still remain significant today.

Since the early twentieth century, many people mobilized to protect the Heijō palace complex and capital. About one hundred years ago, Tanada Kajūrō (1860-1921) devoted himself to a preservation campaign that resulted in the designation of the Heijō palace complex as a National Historic Site.[3] Later, in the postwar period, the site was again in danger of destruction by plans to build a train station or road. But at each juncture, a preservation campaign succeeded in blocking such plans and protecting the ancient ruins.

Today, the Heijō palace ruins serve the community by functioning as a Designated Historical Park, and on weekends and holidays you can see families having picnics there and enjoying themselves. Yet this latest development into a historical park also took place after many years of lobbying and campaigning for which we must be thankful.

In 1998 the Heijō palace ruins, in addition to several other buildings in the vicinity, were established as a UNESCO World Heritage Site, "Historic Monuments of Ancient Nara." Since 2009, plans have been underway for another phase of development to further enhance the site as a National Government Park.

How to manage this important historical site in the best manner possible for the people of today and in the future is a responsibility that falls upon those of us who are now living at the present time.

On this point, a wealth of new knowledge concerning the Heijō palace ruins and Heijōkyō has been unearthed through extensive archaeological survey. A great number of publications and reports have emerged from this large body of material but, among these, very few seem to provide direct answers to simple, basic questions about the

---

[3] For an explanation of specific categories such as National Historic Site or Designated Historical Park, see Yoko Hsueh Shirai, "Public Memory and Identity Politics at the Ruined Buddhist Temple Kudaraji ato in Hirakata City," *Sungkyun Journal of East Asian Studies* 9.2 (2009): 185-211. The article is available online at http://sjeas.skku.edu/upload/200911/185-211%20Yoko.pdf (accessed 27 June 2011).

Heijō palace ruins and the Heijō capital. To this end, and on the occasion of the 1300th anniversary of the transfer of the capital to Heijōkyō, the Archaeological Institute of Kashihara, Nara Prefecture, initiated a project to answer one hundred basic questions in an easily understandable format, hoping to create a reader-friendly book. Instead of focusing on the opulent nature of Tenpyō culture during this period, often represented by the priceless treasures stored at Shōsōin repository at the Buddhist temple Tōdaiji,[4] this book responds to questions that are more relevant to the interests and concerns we now face in our contemporary lives.

If the 100 Questions & Answers that we selected do not exactly match your set of questions, our hope is for the book to serve as a springboard inspiring you to seek out your own answers and learn even more about the Heijō palace ruins, Heijōkyō, and the Nara period as a whole.[5]

Now, let us begin our investigation of the Japanese capital of thirteen hundred years ago.

---

[4] Shōsōin is a storehouse located within the Tōdaiji temple grounds, and treasures both secular and sacred belonging to Heavenly Sovereign Shōmu were placed inside Shōsōin after his death in 756 under the supervision of his Queen-consort, Kōmyō. See Shōsōin Jimusho, eds., *Treasures of the Shōsōin* (Tokyo: Asahi Shinbun, 1965). For details concerning Shōmu and Kōmyō, see Joan R. Piggott, *The Emergence of Japanese Kingship* (Stanford, California: Stanford University Press, 1997). An article by W. Wayne Farris, "Pieces in a Puzzle: Changing Approaches to the Shōsōin Documents," *Monumenta Nipponica* 62.4(2007): 397-436, discusses how the documents inside Shōsōin have been studied by scholars.

[5] The Nara period begins with the transfer of the capital to Nara in 710, and generally ends with the transfer of the capital to Kyoto in 794.

PART ONE:
Transfer of the capital to Heijōkyō begins!

* * *

1 WHICH HEAVENLY SOVEREIGN ISSUED THE EDICT TO TRANSFER THE CAPITAL?

This was none other than Heavenly Sovereign Genmei. On the fifteenth day of the second month of the first year of Wadō (hereafter written as 708.2.15), Genmei issued the edict for *sento* or transfer of the capital. However, the decision to transfer the capital to Heijōkyō was not made by Genmei alone. A year earlier, on 707.2.19, her predecessor, Heavenly Sovereign Monmu convened a session with powerful courtiers to discuss the possibility of *sento*. Unfortunately, Monmu died four months later. Supporters of *sento* continued to debate the merits of a new capital, and courtiers active in these debates presumably influenced Genmei's eventual declaration of *sento*.

One prominent courtier was Fujiwara Fuhito. A month after Genmei issued the *sento* edict Fuhito was promoted from the rank of *dainagon*, a senior counselor, to *udaijin* or Minister of the Right—one of the most powerful ministers at court. *Udaijin* is a deputy of the *sadaijin*, or Minister of the Left, and Isonokami Maro occupied this position. Fujiwara Fuhito later played a central role in the creation of a new system of governance at Heijōkyō, and some scholars believe that the move to Heijōkyō was simply one part of a master plan to bring about such a change.

2 WHAT WAS SIGNIFICANT ABOUT HEIJŌKYŌ?

The Heavenly Sovereign's place of residence and government offices were located at the capital. Yet if the only defining feature or function of the capital was to serve as a place for the Heavenly Sovereign and government officials to live and work, then there would not have been a need to build the capital on such a large and imposing scale. In this case, what role was the Nara capital expected to fulfill?

In order to govern and rule over the Japanese islands, the capital needed to unequivocally exemplify the immense authority of the state, and attempted to do so by presenting a built environment that was imposing, splendid, and beyond comparison. When visitors entered the capital, they were meant to feel overwhelmed and be compelled to obey the rule of law. As for visiting foreign envoys, the appearance of a magnificent capital was intended to reflect the distinguished nature of both the Heavenly Sovereign and the state.

In a certain sense, paying close attention to a capital's visual program during the planning and building stages might be analogous to the way in which modern nation-states compete in a military arms race. Building up an arsenal of weapons is definitely not a good thing, but possessing such weapons can serve to prevent wars from initiating; similarly, an intimidating capital may have prevented rebellions from starting and possibly helped towards securing the authority of rule over the land.

3 WHY WAS HEIJŌKYŌ BUILT AT THIS LOCATION?

When the edict to transfer the capital was issued in 708, the Heijō (Nara) area was deemed a superior location because it accorded well with the principles of *feng shui*, a practice of divination by means of geographic features. The edict stated that the site is in harmony with the four cardinal points symbolized by the *shishin*, or the four deities: Vermillion Bird (south), Azure Dragon (east), White Tiger (west), and the Black Warrior/ Tortoise (north).[6] According to the positive and negative principles of Chinese philosophy, yin and yang, an auspicious location has a mountain range on the north side, a lake on the south, a flowing river on the east, and a road on the west. Possessing all of these geographic features, Heijō was considered a highly suitable location for the new capital.

Heijō was also strategically located on key transportation networks. Situated on the northern extremity of the Nara basin, major rivers and waterways connected Heijōkyō to distant regions. For example, just beyond the mountain Narayama to the north of the capital was the Kizu River. The Kizu merged with the Yodo River, and a boat traveling south down the Yodo would eventually arrive at Naniwa port in Osaka Bay. Ships departing Naniwa could easily reach outlying regions further west. The Kizu River also connected to the Uji River, and travel in a northeasterly direction on this river would bring a boat to massive Biwa Lake, an important gateway to regions farther east.

Establishing an orderly and efficient transportation network linking the capital to distant provinces was important because all kinds of regional goods needed to be shipped to the capital. Heavy, bulky items such as bales of rice or lumber were especially difficult to transport over land. With its choice location, Heijō became a central hub for a water-based transportation network.

---

6   For an English translation of the edict from 708, see J. B. Snellen, "Shoku nihongi (Chronicles of Japan)," *The Transactions of the Asiatic Society of Japan*, 2nd series, 11 (1934): 220.

4 DID ANOTHER CAPITAL SERVE AS A MODEL?

Most scholars agree that Heijōkyō was generally modeled after the Chinese Tang capital, Chang'an. Many of the same basic characteristics are reflected at Heijōkyō: a city based on a rectangular shape with a grid street plan; a palace complex occupying the center of the capital's northern end; and a broad main street, Suzaku Boulevard. Some scholars claim that Heijōkyō was heavily influenced by Chang'an, although the scale was reduced to become one quarter the size of Chang'an.

In the case of Chang'an, much of the city was subdivided into a series of four-sided wards enclosed by high walls, with a gate on each of the four sides. This surface plan made it difficult for people to pass from one ward to another, and served as a means to prevent conflict by segregating the city's multi-ethnic communities and religious groups.[7] One of the essential characteristics of Chang'an is this layout of the city.

However, a similar kind of surface plan was not employed at Heijōkyō. Accordingly, Chang'an and Heijōkyō are fundamentally different. In consideration of this major point of departure, to say that Heijōkyō is an exact replica of Chang'an is an oversimplification. It might be more precise to describe Heijōkyō as a capital that was conscious of, and influenced by, Chang'an.

---

7   According to Nancy Shatzman Steinhardt, *Chinese Imperial City Planning* (Honolulu: University of Hawai'i Press, 1990), 96, "the wards were strictly supervised—their primary function was still population control." Steinhardt's book also offers numerous diagrams and illustrations with regard to Chinese capitals.

5 Before Heijōkyō was built at the site, what was already located there?

Prior to the construction of Heijōkyō, farming villages and rice fields are believed to have occupied the area. Since an earlier date, the government had implemented the *kokugunri* system that divided up land into a series of administrative units, starting with large provinces (*koku*), then counties or districts (*gun*), and finally into villages (*ri*).[8] A major street referred to as Shimotsu michi, which was the predecessor of Suzaku Boulevard at Heijōkyō, served as a border between what had been Soekami County on the east side of the street, and Soejimo County on the west side.

Archaeological surveys in this area recovered evidence of only a few, scattered settlements predating Heijōkyō. One village dating to the second half of the Asuka period was discovered when the environs of Suzaku Boulevard were excavated.[9] Ōno ri or Ōno village was inscribed with black ink on wooden *mokkan* discovered at the site, indicating the name of the *ri*.[10] The sparse settlement of this area was presumably another factor in favor of Heijōkyō's future location, permitting the extensive building campaign to proceed with little disruption.

Historical records indicate that on 708.9.14, Heavenly Sovereign Genmei traveled to an area called Sugawara and paid compensation in the form of bolts of cloth and rice to farmers who had been displaced

---

8   An analogy might be: California as *koku*, Los Angeles County as *gun*, and Hollywood as *ri*.

9   The Asuka period spans from circa 592 to 710 and precedes the Nara period.

10   *Mokkan* are thin strips of wood that served as notepads or inventory slips. Handmade paper was a valuable commodity, and strips of wood were used as everyday writing surfaces. See Joan Piggott, "*Mokkan*: Wooden Documents from the Nara Period," *Monumenta Nipponica* 45.4 (1990): 449-470.

as a result of the Heijōkyō construction project. Even today, Sugawara is the name of an area that is located to the south of the Buddhist temple Saidaiji in Nara city.[11]

---

11 Built to the west of the Heijō palace complex, Saidaiji is still active as a major temple.

6 WERE *KOFUN* (MOUNDED TUMULI) DISPLACED DURING THE BUILDING OF HEIJŌKYŌ?

According to material evidence unearthed by archaeologists, several *kofun* or mounded tumuli were destroyed to build the streets, residences, and palace structures at Heijōkyō.[12] Official policy during the time of construction, however, stipulated that if a burial mound were accidentally excavated by workers then the tomb must be reburied immediately—not abandoned in its exposed state—and proper ritual activity was to be conducted, such as pouring rice wine on the site to appease the spirits of the deceased.

Nonetheless, monumental keyhole-shaped mounded tombs were in fact destroyed to make space for Great Audience Hall (see Figures 2, 3, 4) and various other government buildings at the Heijō palace complex. One such keyhole-shaped tomb is known as Ichiba kofun, measuring two hundred fifty meters in length. The squared front-end of the tomb was destroyed but the circular mound at the rounded back-end of the tomb remains extant. Other keyhole-shaped tombs, such as Shimeno kofun, measuring one hundred meters in length, were completely leveled. As evidence of destroyed burial mounds, broken fragments of clay cylinders called *haniwa* —placed atop mounded tumuli— were found at the palace complex.

Not every tomb, however, was destroyed to make way for the new capital. Hōraisan kofun situated near the Kintetsu Amagatsuji train station, and Nenbutsujiyama kofun located near the Kintetsu Nara train station remained intact. A third example is Sugiyama kofun situated to

---

12 Massive, mounded tombs known as *kofun* were largely built between the middle of the third century and the late seventh century in Japan. See Gina L. Barnes, *State Formation in Japan: Emergence of a 4th-century Ruling Elite* (New York and Oxon: Routledge, 2007).

the north of the temple Daianji, which incorporated the tomb into the temple grounds.

While many *kofun* are thought to have been destroyed during the construction of Heijōkyō, some were left intact as mentioned above and sections from the *kofun*—such as the stone masonry—were sometimes reused to construct new gardens and lakes.

7 HOW MANY PEOPLE WERE INVOLVED IN THE CONSTRUCTION PROJECT?

The transfer of the capital to Heijōkyō required the construction of the Inner Palace within the palace complex where the Heavenly Sovereign resided, in addition to erecting administrative buildings for government officials. A great many people were needed to complete such projects.

Concerning the nature of taxes that were collected at the time, in addition to paying taxes in the form of rice or bolts of cloths, manual labor was also required. Laborers from various regions throughout Japan assembled in the capital to fulfill tax obligations, and were put to work with the task of building Heijōkyō.

For just the Heijō palace complex alone, the preparation of the ground—such as making the ground flat or filling in rice fields—required an estimated three thousand or perhaps sixteen thousand workers per day, depending on which specialist you ask. An accurate count of the people who participated in the construction projects cannot be determined at this time.

As for the nature of the construction work, this seems to have been extremely harsh and physically demanding. Those who could no longer withstand the circumstances and subsequently fled are believed to be quite high in number. To return home, however, was to risk capture and punishment. With nowhere to go, many of the fugitive laborers became vagrants, literally homeless. Each time a person went missing, a replacement laborer had to be sent to the capital from the same hometown.

In this manner, various resources were appropriated to build the capital. A vast number of people are thought to have participated, but the total figure is unknown.

8 WAS THE GEKYŌ SECTION PLANNED FROM THE START?

On the northeastern edge of Heijōkyō, between the horizontally aligned streets Nijō and Gojō, a section of the capital protrudes further eastward. This protruding section is generally referred to as Gekyō (see no.8 in Map 2), but, to be precise, it is actually part of Sakyō (see no.7 in Map 2).[13] Visitors to Nara who disembark at the Kintetsu Nara train station today would find themselves in the Gekyō section of the capital.

Initially, it was believed that Gekyō was a later addition to the rectangular shape of Heijōkyō. However, recent scholarship has demonstrated that the streets and other partitions of Gekyō are in strict agreement with the rest of the capital. In other words, the dominant view now finds that Gekyō was likely planned from the start.

Built at Gekyō were prominent temples like Kōfukuji and Gangōji. Established at a slightly higher elevation, these temples appear to look down at the relatively far Heijō palace to the west. Still a major Buddhist temple today, Kōfukuji was founded to serve as the family temple of the Fujiwara lineage group whose members aggressively supported the transfer of the capital to Heijō. Some scholars even argue that Gekyō was intentionally planned in order to accommodate the construction of Kōfukuji.

---

13 Gekyō literally means "outside the capital." Suzaku Boulevard bisected the capital into two sections, the left side and the right side. The naming system of each side was not based on our perspective as we look at a map of the city, but from the right and left side as seen by the Heavenly Sovereign situated at the palace and looking southward down Suzaku Boulevard. Hence, Sakyō or "left-side of the capital" is located to the east of Suzaku Boulevard, and Ukyō or "right-side of the capital" to the west, contradicting what we would see on a map.

9 HOW LONG DID IT TAKE TO COMPLETE THE TRANSFER OF THE CAPITAL?

Following the *sento* edict on 708.2.15, about two years passed before Genmei moved from the Fujiwara palace to Heijō palace on 710.3.10. At the time of her move only the living quarters or Inner Palace (Dairi) at the palace complex were complete, and construction projects progressed all around her. If other sections of Heijō palace complex— the most significant core of the capital—were unfinished at this point, we can only wonder about the state of completion regarding the rest of the capital.

Because clear evidence exists that Great Audience Hall at the palace complex was finished by 715, it might be reasonable to assume that most of the palace complex had taken shape and was functional by this time. Quite a few more years would pass before the entire capital reached completion, indicating the long and difficult process involved with moving the capital.

10 HOW DID THE TRANSFER OCCUR?

The former capital of Fujiwarakyō was located to the south of Heijōkyō. Accompanying Heavenly Sovereign Genmei, who officially moved to Heijōkyō on 710.3.10, were government officials and their families. Their relocation as a group seems to have taken place both swiftly and decisively because over half of the buildings at Fujiwarakyō disappeared all at once according to the material record.

After arriving at Heijōkyō, officials were allotted a plot of residential land within the capital in accordance with their rank. Homes predominantly built of wood and used at Fujiwarakyō had probably been dismantled, brought to Heijōkyō, and then reassembled at this new location.

Unlike today, there were no professional movers that could help with packing and moving. Each family probably had to load their belongings onto carts and arrange to have the carts transported to Heijōkyō. Of course, moving expenses were not reimbursed. All costs associated with the move had to be paid out-of-pocket.

11 AFTER THE TRANSFER TO HEIJŌKYŌ WAS COMPLETE, WHAT HAPPENED TO THE FORMER CAPITAL FUJIWARAKYŌ?

After Genmei moved out of Fujiwara palace on 710.3.10, Minister of the Left Isonokami Maro stayed behind and was placed in charge of Fujiwarakyō. Major structures from the Fujiwara palace complex, such as Great Audience Hall, were completely dismantled and transported—roof tiles and all—to Heijōkyō. Numerous buildings erected outside the palace complex at Fujiwarakyō, like Buddhist temples, were also transferred.

After the completion of the transfer, Fujiwarakyō was reallocated into standardized units of agricultural land (*jōrisei*) and turned into rice fields. Eventually, all traces of the capital disappeared.

Fujiwarakyō served as the capital for just sixteen years. Apparently this length of time was not enough for people to set down roots and continue living at the site. So with the departure of the Heavenly Sovereign to Heijōkyō, the inhabitants of Fujiwarakyō followed suit. A city that was artificially created to serve as a political center might be destined to meet this kind of end, as opposed to settlements that are self-propagating and arise naturally in a certain sense.

PART TWO:
LIFE IN THE PALACE COMPLEX AT HEIJŌKYŌ

* * *

12 WHAT WAS THE PALACE COMPLEX CALLED?

The official chronicles of this period, *Shoku nihongi*, were written using Chinese characters. Chinese characters for both Heijōkyō (the capital) and Heijōkyū (the palace complex) appear in the historical annals, but since *Shoku nihongi* was edited and completed during a later period— the Heian period—it is unclear whether these two terms had been employed during the early eighth century or were later additions.[14]

There is, however, something called *senmyō* which is like a transcript of the Heavenly Sovereign's speech. The editors of *Shoku nihongi* probably did not alter or revise *senmyō*. Since there are references to the Heijō palace complex in *senmyō*, it is quite certain that the Chinese characters for Heijōkyū were used during the eighth century.

Because the Heavenly Sovereign resided at only one palace on a daily basis, the Heijō palace may have been simply called "the palace" (*miya*), similar to how the current *tennō* residence at Tokyo is referred to as *kōkyo*.

If we know how the palace complex was transcribed in the documentary sources, what about the pronunciation? In the collection of poems *Man'yōshū*, one poem refers to the capital as *Nara no miyako*.[15] It is important to keep in mind that an inconsistent use of Chinese char-

14 The Heian period begins with the transfer of the capital to Heian (Kyoto) in 794, and generally ends in 1185 or 1192.

15 *Manyōshū* or "Collection of Ten Thousand Leaves" was compiled during the Nara period and contains about 4500 poems. For an English translation of selected poems, see Japanese Classics Translation Committee, eds., *1000 Poems from the Manyōshū: The Complete Nippon Gakujutsu Shinkokai Translation* (Mineola, New York: Dover Publications, 2005), which is a slightly abridged re-publication of the original 1940 edition published by Iwanami Shoten, Tokyo. Documents transcribed during the seventh and eighth centuries in Japan often used different Chinese characters to signify the same entity, especially for the names of people or places. Part of the reason may be due to the nature of how things were transcribed. Since Chinese script was employed to correspond to a spoken Japanese word, although the pronunciation remained constant, an individual's choice in how to transcribe the word fluctuated during this early period of writing.

acters referring to the same subject is evident among various poems written by different authors; that is, different authors used different Chinese characters to signify *Nara*. At any rate, if the capital was known as *Nara no miyako* then the palace complex may have been called *Nara no miya*.

13 WHAT WERE SOME OF THE ANNUAL TRADITIONS AND HOLIDAYS?

Among the annual rites celebrated at Heijōkyō were *setsujitsu* falling on the dates 1.1 (first month.first day), 1.7, 1.16, 3.3, 5.5, 7.7, and certain days in the eleventh month. *Setsujitsu* were holidays celebrating seasonal changes. A royal banquet, *sechie*, was also held.

On the first day of the first month (1.1) of a new year, a ritual ceremony called *chōga* took place at Great Audience Hall. The Heavenly Sovereign received felicitations for the new year from well-wishers. Courtiers living at the capital participated in the ceremony, as well as those bearing gifts from distant provinces in the northeast and southern Kyūshū. Foreign emissaries often arrived from the kingdoms of Unified Silla and Parhae on the Korean peninsula.

The officials assembled in rows at the expansive outdoor plaza facing Great Audience Hall, where raised banners illustrated with an image of a bird, sun, azure dragon, vermillion bird, moon, black warrior/turtle, or white tiger fluttered in the wind.

Music was played, dances were performed, and gifts of rare, auspicious animals—white foxes, pigeons, pheasants, turtles, mice, or swallows—were given to the Heavenly Sovereign.

14 WHAT KINDS OF JOBS DID PEOPLE HAVE AT THE HEIJŌ PALACE COMPLEX?

The Heijō palace complex was part of Heijōkyō, and situated inside the Heijō palace complex was the Heavenly Sovereign's residence, official meeting places such as Great Audience Hall, and numerous government offices. If you visit Tokyo today, you can view a similar layout with the Imperial Palace located adjacent to numerous government ministries at Kasumigaseki. During the Nara period, the Heavenly Sovereign participated in state rituals and received foreign emissaries at Great Audience Hall, while government officials managed census registers (*koseki*), tax payments, and performed other kinds of administrative duties at the government offices.

Heijōkyō was intended, in part, to serve as a place to house the government officials who worked at the palace complex. When registering their personal census record, some officials listed Heijōkyō as their permanent place of residence but most officials registered their home province outside the capital as their permanent domicile. For these officials, living at Heijōkyō was something like a temporary job transfer and not a permanent move.

Aside from government officials, who were predominantly male, female attendants also served the Heavenly Sovereign and Queen-consort inside the palace complex. Another group of people entering the palace complex on a daily basis were students learning about astronomy, devising a calendar, or the practice of medicine.

Early each morning, untold numbers of people waited for the monumental Suzaku Gate to open—the main entrance to the palace complex—in order to get to work. The surrounding streets near Suzaku Gate must have been highly congested and jam-packed with busy commuters.

15 WHAT KINDS OF MUSICAL INSTRUMENTS WERE PLAYED AT THE PALACE COMPLEX?

Some of the musical instruments played at the palace complex were stored inside Shōsōin repository and have survived to the present day. There are instruments originating from what are now the countries of Iran, India, China, and Korea.

The Shōsōin instruments can be divided into three groups: percussion instruments played by hitting their surfaces or shaking them (*kuretsuzumi, niko*), stringed instruments played by causing the taut strings to vibrate (*wagon, kin, sō, shiragigoto, biwa, kugo, genkan*), and wind instruments sounded by blowing air into them (*shakuhachi, yokobue*).

An especially noteworthy and rare instrument, known as *raden shitan gogen biwa*, is a five-stringed *biwa* lute made of red sandalwood with an elaborate mother-of-pearl inlay. Believed to originate from India, the instrument stored inside Shōsōin appears to be the only remaining one of its kind.

Another stringed instrument, the *shiragigoto*, this type of instrument is considered to be an early prototype of the *kayakin* that is still in use today at Korea.

Musical instruments used to make music in Tang China (*niko, kin, sō, biwa, genkan, shakuhachi, yokobue*) are the most numerous among those stored at Shōsōin. This indicates that Chinese-inspired music was frequently played at the Heijō palace complex and at Tōdaiji (the Buddhist temple complex that houses Shōsōin repository), informing us of the very cosmopolitan nature of the capital.

PART THREE:
THE INHABITANTS
OF HEIJŌKYŌ

* * *

16 DID SOME PEOPLE MOVE TO HEIJŌKYŌ FROM FARAWAY PLACES?

Heijōkyō was inhabited by the Heavenly Sovereign, members of the royal family, aristocrats, Buddhist clergy, commoners, and low-ranking bound servants (*nuhi*). Over half of these people originated from the Kinai region, consisting of the group of provinces lying closest to Heijōkyō and also known as the home provinces. Specifically, these were the provinces of Yamato, Kawachi, Settsu, Yamashiro, and Izumi.

From outside the home provinces came the sons and younger brothers of provincial administrators. These young men were sent to the capital to serve as *hyōe*, charged with policing Heijōkyō. Also serving to guard the palace and capital were *eji*, troops assembled from among the conscripts of various provincial regiments. These guards did not assume permanent posts at the capital but were on rotation, taking turns to serve at Heijōkyō.

In addition to those who came to serve as security forces at the capital, many others were forcibly dispatched to the capital and assigned to work at the government offices, often performing menial tasks or engaging in construction work. Still others journeyed to the capital in order to deliver the various goods and taxes-in-kind that were assessed to each district.

As a result, men and women from all over Japan were living at Heijōkyō. Persons of diverse social standing came from various places, near and far, and assembled at one location—this was the essential character of Heijōkyō.

17 WHAT KINDS OF JOBS WERE AVAILABLE TO RESIDENTS OF HEIJŌKYŌ?

Most of the people living at Heijōkyō were government officials who worked at the palace. However, some were employed outside the palace. Grand, aristocratic households, for instance, employed many people. Itō Yōkadō Nara, a multilevel shopping mall, currently occupies the site where the stately Nagayaō or Prince Nagaya residence once existed (see no.11 in Map 2). Several hundred people are thought to have worked at the Nagayaō residence doing all sorts of jobs: building maintenance; acquisition and harvesting of grains and vegetables; food preparation; water usage; and overseeing physicians and the medicine supply. Aside from administrators, there were specialized artisans who might be in charge of applying dyes to clothing, landscaping, or taking care of the horses, dogs, and chickens.

Aside from secular households, numerous Buddhist temples located inside Heijōkyō were served by a large population of resident monastic clergy. Assisting with the building of such temples were specialized guilds or workshops that both constructed the temples and manufactured religious icons.

The large, state-run markets at the capital were another source of employment. Merchants selling their wares at market stalls and referred to as *ichibito* engaged in commerce as their occupation.

Still others were mobilized from various provinces located outside the capital and worked in a more physically demanding capacity, perhaps as security forces or as construction workers.

18 WHAT WAS THE POPULATION?

Despite the census registers that had been established by the Nara period, there are no documentary records indicating the exact population of Heijōkyō. As a result, scholars use various sources to provide a reasonable estimate.

One scholar, Sawada Goichi, compared the population of Heijōkyō with that of modern Kanazawa city and also analyzed a legal document from the year 773 that listed the total number of elderly persons residing at Heijōkyō. Sawada proposed that approximately two hundred thousand people inhabited the capital, and his figure was treated as a reliable estimate for a long time.

However, in recent years some researchers used the population at Fujiwarakyō as a reference and proposed a Heijōkyō population of seventy-four thousand. Other specialists analyzed the total residential area within the capital to suggest a population of sixty-two thousand. In light of such developments, it seems that even after accounting for substantial population growth over time, the population was unlikely to have exceeded one hundred thousand at Heijōkyō.

To be precise, the population figure accounted for only those who fell into the category of *kyōko*, consisting only of households residing on officially registered Heijōkyō property. Each of these households received an allotment of rice fields from the state (*kubunden*), but the fields were located outside the capital. If some of the households set out to cultivate their fields and ended up leaving the capital to settle nearby, the Heijōkyō population would subsequently decrease over time.

Another important factor to consider is the fluctuation inherent in large metropolitan areas. Around the time when tax payments were due, many people traveled to the capital to submit their taxes, temporarily inflating the population. With large waves of people coming in and out of the capital, this aspect of Heijōkyō resembles the cities of Tokyo and Osaka today.

19 WHAT WAS THE RATIO OF MEN TO WOMEN?

Documentary records from the contemporary period provide a general idea of how many government officials and monastic clergy inhabited the city. Assuming that the Heijōkyō population was around one hundred thousand people, roughly forty thousand—or 40 percent of the entire population—were government officials or part of the monastic clergy. As for the number of women who worked as government officials, the state employed about three hundred women to serve the Queen-consort. If you look at this figure, it becomes evident that the vast majority of officials were men. Clearly, the palace complex was a male-dominated society.

As for the rest of the population, surviving partial records of a population registry known as *keichō* inform us that the ratio of men to women was about equal. Accordingly, the overall ratio of men to women at Heijōkyō might have been 6:4, but cannot be confirmed.

20 WHAT WAS THE AVERAGE LIFE EXPECTANCY?

In present-day Japan the average life expectancy is more than eighty years of age, and longevity rates are among the highest in the world. Although precise figures cannot be determined, for someone living during the time of the Heijō capital the average life expectancy was significantly lower than what it is today.

To find out what the life expectancy may have been during the time of the Heijō capital, specialists often analyze human remains or bones. Unfortunately, very few human remains dating to this period have been unearthed. As another means to establish how long people lived, calculations are made from surviving written records such as census registers. Based on these records, the average life expectancy is speculated to be around twenty years of age.

It is important to keep in mind, however, that these census records were taken from people living outside the capital, in the outlying peripheral regions; for this reason, the longevity rate does not exactly reflect the average lifespan of someone who lived at Heijōkyō. Given that the Heavenly Sovereign and aristocrats living at Heijōkyō had easy access to food which was both plentiful and of higher nutritional value than what was consumed by the general population, mortality rates were affected as well. Specifically, the average life expectancy for a Heavenly Sovereign is close to sixty years of age, and written accounts provide details of an aristocrat who lived to about eighty years of age. In light of such varying degrees of life expectancy, the average life expectancy for Heijōkyō residents was probably somewhat higher than the overall average.

21 WHAT WAS THE FAMILY STRUCTURE LIKE?

In the not-so-distant past, many families in Japan consisted of three generations living together: parents, their children, and grandparents. Traditional families now generally include a husband, wife, and children. With the declining birth rate in recent years, a typical family might consist of three or four persons.

In contrast to the small size of a modern family, families during the time of Heijōkyō were large and included not just the parents, children, and other relatives, but also *nuhi* or low-ranking bound servants who lived at the same residence. In this fashion, the definition of who belonged to a family was much broader in comparison to today.

Family registries of some of the commoners who resided at Heijōkyō still survive, and while one family registered ten people, the average family size at Heijōkyō appears to have been six or seven people.

22 WAS A COMMON LANGUAGE SPOKEN?

Based on documentary records dating to the Nara period and earlier, government officials who traveled to the extreme northeast (Tōhoku chihō) and southwest (Kyūshū nanbu) regions were accompanied by translators called *osa*, indicating substantial variation among the regional dialects.

Because people originating from all over Japan commingled at the capital, you might assume that a number of dialects circulated at Heijōkyō as well.

Yet if this was the prevailing situation, it would have been difficult for administrators to manage the city and keep it functioning. For instance, providing critical and specific instructions to workers at a construction site would have been nearly impossible. Co-workers and colleagues would not have been able to chat or gossip while on the job. In essence, Heijōkyō residents faced a relatively sudden and urgent need to communicate with each other on a wide scale. Some scholars believe that a common language rapidly came into existence during this period, the genesis of what later developed into the Japanese language.

It could be said that the most significant contribution resulting from the creation of Heijōkyō was the development of a common, Japanese language.

PART FOUR:
DAILY LIFE AT HEIJŌKYŌ

* * *

23 WHAT WERE HOMES LIKE?

Residential land at Heijōkyō was allocated to each resident, and the nature of each allotment reflected that person's social status and rank. Someone with high rank would receive a large allotment of land, and someone with low rank a much smaller allotment. Archaeological survey results also inform us that residences taking up large plots of land were situated near the palace complex, while small plots were located farther away.

Regarding the plots allotted to the general population, a rectangular ward—measuring about 133 meters on each side (about 14,400 square meters) —was subdivided into sixteen units (about 900 square meters each). In the case of a low-ranking government official, one of these units would be further divided in half (450 square meters). Others received plots of land that were even smaller than 450 square meters.

Built within each plot was the main and largest building, the *shuoku*, often followed by the construction of one or two smaller buildings, *fukuoku*, in addition to a well for water. When erecting a building, wooden pillars were first buried in the ground in what is known as the *hottate bashira* style. Next, walls built of wooden planks were installed. Roofing material was either wood board (*itabuki*) or thatch (*kayabuki*). Homes were basic and constructed simply. In relation to the total amount of allotted land, the size of a building was quite small; since many people are speculated to have lived inside each home, the environment would not have been exactly pleasant.

24 FROM SUNRISE TO SUNSET, WHAT DID A GOVERNMENT OFFICIAL DO ALL DAY?

A government official working at the palace complex started work at daybreak. Since the sun rises at different times during the year, the work schedule likewise shifted accordingly. Telling time was the job of *rōkoku hakase* who were government officials employed at the Onmyōryō or the Divination Bureau.

The *rōkoku hakase* read a clock that was driven by a series of water movements. At their order, a drum would be beaten or large bell sounded to indicate a certain time. Upon hearing these sounds and learning the time, officials left for work on horseback or walked to the palace complex.

While high-ranking officials lived close to the palace complex, low-ranking officials commuted from far away, generally between two and four kilometers from the palace. This meant that low-ranking officials needed to wake up earlier since being late to work meant the gate would close and they could no longer enter the workplace.

Officials were only paid to work during morning hours, but were expected to stay late into the day doing additional work as overtime. Yet unlike today, there was no such thing as overtime pay. It was time for the officials to return home when night fell.

The state-run marketplace did not open for business until the afternoon, based on the premise that government officials finished their work by noon and could shop afterwards.

Aside from government officials, other residents of the capital also started work at dawn and went to sleep with the setting sun. Without the modern convenience of artificial lighting, the people of Heijōkyō adjusted their lives to coincide with the movement of the sun.

25 HOW DID PEOPLE TELL TIME?

The Divination Bureau at the Heijō palace complex was a government institution devoted to astronomical observation, calculating calendars, and divination by means of geographic features. Another function was to manage the clock based on water movements and to announce the time.

Managing the clock required constant attention, both day and night, and two specialists were charged with this task. These two specialists probably took turns, with one present during each shift. Serving the specialists were twenty assistants who were divided into two groups, with ten people in each group. Time was announced to Heijōkyō inhabitants by sounding a drum or large bell loudly.

Time was important at the Heijō palace complex since punctuality, whether in starting the workday or opening up the marketplace, was essential.

The creation of the first water clock in Japan is attributed to Prince Nakanoōe, who later reigned as Heavenly Sovereign Tenji. This happened in 660. Material evidence of the water clock was discovered at a site identified as Mizuochi iseki in Asukamura, Nara prefecture. Following the establishment of this clock the practice of structuring a day in accordance with measured, standardized time was set into motion. In other words, a way of life dictated by time started during this period in Japan.

Regardless of the significant role that time-keeping played at the capital, no one else outside Heijōkyō—with the exception of a limited number of provincial administrators—had any need to know the exact time. These people probably managed their day according to the movement of the sun.

26 WHAT KIND OF CALENDAR WAS USED?

Given that the Heavenly Sovereign was credited with introducing the measurement of time and the calculation of calendars, such practices came to represent the authority of the Heavenly Sovereign who still, in symbolic terms, presided over their management.

During the eleventh month of each year, a new calendar for the upcoming year was created by the Divination Bureau and distributed to government offices. Officials would then copy and distribute the calendar on a wider scale.

Calendars were calculated by using a cyclic numeral system of sixty different combinations, known as the sexagenary cycle or *kanshi*. The specific combination for a certain day was associated with good or bad fortune, so the calendar contained notations as to which days were lucky or not. These calendars were called *guchūreki*.

According to the material record, calendars were made and used prior to the Nara period. That is, recovered at the palace complex of the previous capital, Fujiwarakyō, was a *mokkan* or wooden document inscribed with a request for additional writing brushes to copy a calendar. In addition, an actual *guchūreki* was excavated nearby at the Ishigami iseki site in Asukamura, indicating that this sort of calendar was already in existence since the second half of the Asuka period.

Not only were calendars used at the capital, copies seem to have been widely dispersed in the peripheral regions. One fragment of a calendar was recovered by archaeologists in the Tōhoku region, located to the far north. Accurate dates were also written on wooden inventory tags accompanying products serving as taxes-in-kind and shipped from the provinces to the capital; without a calendar, inscribing dates would have been difficult.

27 WHAT CRIMES DID PEOPLE COMMIT?

The crimes of murder, assault, burglary, and theft occur always, regardless of time or place.

If we fall victim to crime today, we would seek out the police and file a report. Yet if something was stolen during the Nara period, the victim had to personally attempt its recovery. Evidence of such action has been found in the material record, including the excavation of a sign at Heijōkyō that sought the return of a stolen cow. From among the documents stored at Shōsōin repository, an official submitted a request for a leave of absence to search for a stolen item.

The state established a list of eight crimes (Hachigyaku) that were prohibited by law. Some were political in nature, such as revolting against the government. Political crimes were considered to be especially subversive as they threatened the security and authority of the state. Although some crimes committed by criminals might be pardoned in special cases, committing one of the eight abuses was not tolerated.

A list of misdemeanors from this period can be found in a ritual prayer read aloud during a ceremony to ritually purify the royal court. Ōharae took place on the last day of the sixth and twelfth months, and the prayer condemned as crimes the acts of destroying the raised banks of rice fields, filling in drainage ditches, damaging gutters, or scattering manure. While these crimes are largely agricultural in nature, harsh punishment certainly awaited those who committed such transgressions.

28 How were crimes punished?

The Taihō Codes (Taihō ritsuryō) refer to the following punishments: *chi* (beating the buttocks with a bamboo cane), *jō* (beating the buttocks with a rod), *zu* (imprisonment), *ru* (banishment), and *shi* (death penalty). Specific details appear in a set of laws called Gokuryō. In addition to *chi, jō, zu, ru,* and *shi,* aristocratic titles could be stripped, government jobs revoked, and social status demoted. Even a person's name might be changed as a punitive measure.

As one example, in 769 a person named Waké Kiyomaro was punished after returning with a divine message from the oracle at Usa Hachiman shrine that was received unfavorably at court. His name was changed to Wakébe Kitanamaro.[16]

Prisons were also established within Heijōkyō, and there are numerous references to Heijō prison in *Shoku nihongi*. According to one *Shoku nihongi* entry, Heavenly Sovereign Shōmu heard a sad scream emanating from inside the prison at the capital.

One place where penalties were inflicted was the marketplace. Since many people congregated at the marketplace, this was an ideal place to publicly display justice being served; such a display sent a harsh warning to the populace about committing a certain crime.

---

16 The name Wakebe Kitanamaro has various derogatory and offensive characteristics, but most prominent is the use of *kitana* to substitute for *kiyo*; the character for *kitana* means "polluted" or "dirty," while *kiyo* means "pure."

29 WHAT WAS THE CITY LIKE IN THE DEAD OF NIGHT?

Browse through Nara-period laws and you might notice that going out at night was essentially forbidden. Archaeologists discovered traces of small huts illuminated by firelight on Heijōkyō streets, and believe *eji* serving as sentries had occupied the huts while on the lookout for illegal nighttime trespassers.

Anyone who passed by a sentry was probably stopped and questioned about where they were employed, and their current position at work. If an acceptable response was provided, the passerby was likely released; if the response was unacceptable, the person may have been tied up and detained.

If this scenario accurately portrays the capital at night, the implication is that Heijōkyō was constantly under heavy surveillance. Around this time an increasing number of people fled the capital—possibly unable to bear the severe working conditions—and the situation was turning into a big problem. As a means to remedy the problem, a nighttime curfew was likely enforced.

Yet in practice, getting past the guards and fleeing the capital should not have been too difficult, especially since the perimeter of the capital was not enclosed by high walls or *rajō*. Such walls were only built in the vicinity of the southern gateway to the capital, Rajōmon or Rajō Gate (see no.5 in Map 2). As is often the case in Japan, the situation mentioned above might reflect the inherent tension between a somewhat idealized, official policy (*tatemae*) and actual reality.

30 WAS THERE GRAFFITI?

One phenomenon remaining unchanged since ancient times is a person doodling on the margins of a writing surface when taking a quick break from studying or doing work. Archaeologists excavating Heijōkyō often discover wooden documents (*mokkan*) inscribed with a drawing or caricature of a person's face.

One sketch was found among the documents stored at Shōsōin repository. Drawn using black ink, a bearded government official is portrayed with eyes opened so wide that they bulge out of their sockets. His brows are furrowed and the mouth is open to suggest he is angry and possibly yelling. Three Chinese characters indicating "big big discussion" (*daidairon*) appear just above the figure's head, serving to inform us that this man was engaged in a heated discussion with presumably another official, and was making a desperate attempt to assert his own position. Perhaps a nearby colleague decided to make this quick sketch. Similar kinds of sketches, likely made by craftsmen, remain extant on the ceilings at Hōryūji Golden Hall and Pagoda.

In addition to caricatures, there were other sorts of pictures—but these are inappropriate to describe in this book. Obscene images of this sort were usually restricted to hidden places at Heijōkyō such as the unexposed, undersurface of rooftops.

At some of our cities today, you might see graffiti spray-painted on public buildings. If something like this were to happen at Heijōkyō, such as defacing the white earthen walls at the palace complex, the ever-vigilant *eji* would swiftly apprehend the transgressor.

31 WHAT WERE TOILETS LIKE?

Remains of toilets have been identified at a number of excavation sites at Heijōkyō. Apparently, there were two basic types of toilets.

One type was a hole in the ground. After digging a large cavity, a series of wood boards were placed around the top of the hole. Two parallel boards might have been spaced apart just wide enough so that there was ample space between the boards, but close enough to allow a person to comfortably place one foot on each board before squatting. Archaeologists proposed this type of toilet after unearthing large deposits in the ground filled with flat wooden strips called *chūgi*— which likely functioned as a kind of toilet paper—in addition to melon seeds (as evidence of human waste) and shed pupal casings left behind by maggots turning into flies.

Another type of toilet was a flush toilet. Running water was directed into a home by wooden pipes, diverting water from the sewer system running along the side of a street. This water was then redirected from the home to the street gutters.

When the first type of toilet became full, the contents were emptied out and the waste products likely disposed into the street gutters or a nearby river. With raw sewage flowing through the waterways at Heijōkyō, a terrible odor must have permeated the capital. Given this unsanitary and unhygienic environment, after the outbreak of an infectious disease the sickness spread widely and quickly across the population.

On a different note, careful investigation of the accumulated earthen material from ancient toilets allows researchers to learn about the kinds of foods that were consumed, as well as overall standards of health and well-being at the time.

32 WAS THERE TOILET PAPER?

Paper was available during the Nara period, but it was a valuable commodity. Paper was reserved for the preparation of official documents such as census registers, and even wastepaper discarded by government offices was sold at the marketplace.

Under these circumstances, paper was not used as toilet paper. Instead, a thin and flat strip of wood approximately twenty to thirty centimenters in length called *chūgi* functioned in much the same way. Some researchers propose that *mokkan*, which was used as a writing tablet, was somehow appropriated and adapted to become *chūgi*.

Common use of toilet paper in Japan did not begin until after the Pacific War and became widespread after the period of high economic growth. At the present time the quality and size of a sheet of toilet paper is not standardized around the world, and might serve as an indicator of a nation's cultural and living standards.

33 DID PEOPLE TAKE BATHS?

During the Nara period, people generally did not shower or bathe as part of a daily routine.

There were, however, natural hot springs. Taking a dip in the warm, mineral-rich waters was believed to help cure illnesses and heal the body. Asuka-period entries from the historical annals *Nihon shoki* describe the Heavenly Sovereign visiting hot springs at Arima, Dōgo, and Shirahama.[17] The ensuing *Shoku nihongi* annals include a record of Heavenly Sovereign Monmu traveling to the hot springs at Shirahama.

Aside from naturally occurring hot springs found outdoors, places for bathing were also built at the capital and vaguely resemble the baths in Japan today. According to documents stored at Shōsōin repository, there was a *yuya* or "bathing place" at the Office of Scripture Reproduction (Shakyōsho). While wearing a garment called *yukatabira*, the person entered the *yuya* to ritually purify the body before starting work at the Office of Scripture Reproduction, a place where scribes copied Buddhist scriptures to either make duplicate copies for distribution or to generate Buddhist merit through the physical act of replicating the sacred texts.

Also used during this time was a kind of steam bath, not unlike a sauna you might see now. According to a famous legend, Queen-consort Kōmyō established a steam bath at the temple Hokkeji, located adjacent to the palace complex (see no.19 in Map 2), and helped poor and sick commoners benefit from the presumed medicinal properties of a steam bath. A steam bath still remains at Hokkeji, although the present building dates to the Edo period.

---

17 *Nihon shoki* was compiled in 720 but includes records from a much earlier period, some of which are mythological in nature and historically inaccurate. For a complete translation in English, see Aston, W.G., *Nihongi: Chronicles of Japan from the Earliest Times to A.D. 697*, 2 vols, reprint, (Vermont & Tokyo: Charles E. Tuttle Co., 1896/1972).

According to Nara-period temple inventory lists, Tōdaiji, Daianji, and Hōryūji each had a *yuya*. *Yuya* are still extant at Tōdaiji, Hōryūji, and Kōfukuji, although the present buildings postdate the Nara period.

34 COULD MOST PEOPLE TAKE A TRIP TO SEE THE OCEAN?

The majority of Heijōkyō residents probably had very little opportunity to see the ocean. Traveling on vacation was not customary during the Nara period, and only a small, privileged minority possessed the economic resources necessary to take a trip for several days. Certainly there were those who traveled to the capital to submit taxes or fulfill other obligations. Yet some of these people were unable to raise enough funds to pay for their way back home and resorted to living around the periphery of Heijōkyō. In this fashion, traveling was fraught with risk.

From the perspective of the state, the free and unauthorized movement of people from one location to another was inconvenient and destabilizing. In order to properly assess individuals and calculate their tax burden, it was critical that the government account for each individual taxpayer and know the specific location of that individual. For this reason, whenever a person was required to travel in order to make tax payments, a special *mokkan* serving as a travel document was issued.

Under these circumstances, it is hard to imagine that the general population of Heijōkyō could take a seaside trip.

However, even if personally traveling to the ocean may have been a rarity, stories about the sea may have been in circulation because the capital was populated by seasoned travelers. For example, there were officials who had been dispatched to distant provinces, shippers who transported taxes from far away, and foreign envoys who journeyed abroad to places like Tang China.

35 What kind of transportation network connected Heijōkyō to the rest of Japan?

All transportation routes originated from Heijōkyō during the Nara period. Routes to places located east of the capital were the Tōkaidō, Tōsandō, and Hokurikudō. The Tōkaidō largely stretched alongside the eastern coastline (Pacific Ocean), and the Tōsandō passed through the central, inland regions to arrive at the Tōhoku region in the northeast. The Hokurikudō proceeded along the northern coastline (Sea of Japan), and went as far north as present-day Niigata prefecture.

Routes to places located west of the capital were the Sanyōdō, San'indō, Nankaidō, and Saikaidō. The Sanyōdō passed along the coastline of the Seto Inland Sea and was the most critical route as it linked the capital to Dazaifu in Kyūshū—an administrative center and staging area for both the sending and receiving of foreign missions. The San'indō ran along the southern coastline of the Sea of Japan, the Nankaidō connected the capital to Shikoku in the southwest, and the Saikaidō linked Dazaifu to various other locations within Kyūshū.

All of these official circuits were based on preexisting routes, but during the Nara period the roads were straightened and widened to measure about twelve meters across. Further, official post stations known as *umaya* were established at intervals along the routes about sixteen kilometers apart. Horses and provisions were kept at each station and formed a relay system using fast riders on horseback, allowing officials in the capital and provinces to send out important messages in an efficient, timely manner. In a certain sense, the ancient circuits functioned as a kind of information highway.

36 DID A SOCIAL WELFARE SYSTEM EXIST?

In our modern era the government-sponsored social welfare system assists children, the elderly, and those suffering from illness or affected by major natural disasters. No system of this sort existed during the Nara period.

Yet virtuous behavior and doing good works were a significant part of Confucian and Buddhist teachings, so the Heavenly Sovereign and Queen-consort often provided assistance to sick people, children, and the elderly. For example, according to Nara-period laws, persons over the age of sixty were no longer required to submit tax payments, while those over the age of seventy received food assistance. Regions devastated by natural disasters or famine were also exempted from paying taxes for a specific period of time and might receive food assistance from the state.

Especially notable is Queen-consort Kōmyō, a strong supporter of Buddhism who sought to acquire Buddhist merit by performing many good deeds. Kōmyō is reputed to have constructed medicine dispensaries, distributed food to the sick, and established steam baths as places for healing.

As preparation against natural disasters and disease epidemics, storehouses called *gisō* were stocked with emergency food supplies. Yet unlike today, government aid was limited to a small, priviledged minority and did not extend to the general population in the event of a disaster.

37 WHERE WERE GRAVES LOCATED?

Graves were prohibited at Heijōkyō, and not a single grave has been unearthed by archaeologists within the capital. Instead, graves were established on hillsides located to the north, east, and west of Heijōkyō. The gravesites of many high-ranking individuals, including the Heavenly Sovereigns Genmei and Shōmu, were established at the mountains situated to the north—Sahoyama and Nahoyama. Located at the hillsides to the east is the grave of Ō Yasumaro, compiler of *Kojiki*.[18] Also on the east side, near the mountain Ikomayama, are the graves of Gyōki and Prince Nagaya.

What about the graves of commoners? Bodies wrapped in straw mat were found in an ancient riverbed at an excavation site located to the south of Heijōkyō, Hieda iseki in Yamato Kōriyama city. This discovery leads to the possibility that after preparing a corpse by wrapping in straw mat, the body was simply released into the river.

---

18 Completed in 712, *Kojiki* includes origination myths pertaining to the founding of Japan.

38 WHAT KINDS OF DOMESTICATED ANIMALS WERE RAISED?

Horses, cows, dogs, and hawks were raised during the Nara period. Some were work animals, like cows that plowed fields and pulled special carts carrying aristocrats.

Inscribed on a wooden document discovered at the Prince Nagaya residence was a request for food to feed the dogs and cranes. Opinions vary as to whether these animals were kept as pets or were raised to be eaten by people. Hawks were raised for the purpose of hawking, a kind of sport involving the use of raptors to catch wild game.

Archaeologists who excavated Heijōkyō found the bones of various animals—including cows, horses, dogs, wild boars, and deer—accumulated at street gutters and inside wells. Researchers believe some of these animals were used during sacrificial rituals to pray for rain or a bountiful harvest (Gokoku hōjō), while others were killed at workshops for their skins and bones. As a third possibility, some of the animals might have simply died and were placed by their owners at the street gutters.

PART FIVE:
EATING AT HEIJŌKYŌ

* * *

39 HOW WAS FOOD OBTAINED?

Aristocrats and government officials received stipends and income in the form of food products; these products were submitted from all over Japan in payment of taxes. Foods included rice, vegetables, fish, and seasonings.

The range and quantity of food provided to persons living at Heijōkyō was strictly regulated according to the recipient's status and rank. For aristocrats and high-ranking officials, a large variety of food was distributed in ample portions. As a result, many dishes and entrees were prepared at their households.

Aside from the food products provided by the state, this small minority of wealthy households with extensive land allotments cultivated food at their own fields, gardens, and orchards. The wealthy could also purchase additional food at the marketplace.

As for low-ranking officials and the general population, the variety and amount of food distributed to them was incomparably meager in comparison to those at the top of the hierarchy. Commoners generally could not afford marketplace prices and instead grew vegetables on their residential plot of land. A typical meal for commoners often consisted of unpolished brown rice, soup, and perhaps one main dish—or no main dish—which was quite sparse.

40 WHAT ABOUT DRINKING WATER?

Since the earliest times in Japan, notably the Jōmon and Yayoi periods, settlements were built at sites with easy access to water.

However, in the case of a large city like Heijōkyō, securing drinking water became more difficult. Unlike Japan's modern cities that provide safe drinking water to all households, Heijōkyō residents obtained drinking water by digging their own wells.

When constructing a well, the bottom might be lined with gravel or a curved appendage might be used to help clear and purify the water. Many inventive devices were installed by Heijōkyō residents to help secure an important resource, clean drinking water.

41 WHAT WAS THE STAPLE FOOD?

Even during the time of the Heijō capital, rice was the staple food. However, polished white rice was not available for consumption by all residents of Heijōkyō. Only the highest-status individuals at Heijōkyō received distributions of polished white rice from the state; a person's rank determined exactly how much rice they were allowed.

The majority of Heijōkyō residents subsisted on unpolished brown rice, what today is called *genmai*. Yet farmers, who actually cultivated and harvested the rice, were not allowed to eat even brown rice. Instead, they consumed several varieties of millet and other grains (*Setaria italica, Panicum miliaceum, Echinochloa crus-galli*) as their staple food.

Based on estimates of maximum rice yields during the Nara period, the annual rice harvest appears to have been insufficient to feed the entire population for one year and might explain the severe restrictions placed on who was allowed to eat rice.

42 WHAT VARIETIES OF MEAT AND FISH WERE EATEN?

From aristocrats to commoners, the main meat source was wild deer and boar. Cows and horses were not food animals but were highly valued as a source of labor in the fields, as well as transportation for people and freight. Only domestic animals that were very old or injured may have been eaten.

On the more unusual side, written records describe the consumption of monkeys and dogs, which might be difficult to imagine today. Other animals that served as a food source were chicken and wild birds such as pheasant and duck.

During the time of the Heijō capital, and in agreement with Buddhist teachings, the government issued prohibitions against the killing of animals on several occasions. Conversely, the repetition of this prohibition indicates that hunting and consuming animals occurred quite frequently.

Fish caught at the ocean included bonito, tuna, and sea bream, while fish from freshwater lakes and rivers included sweetfish, eel, and salmon.

Because Heijōkyō was not situated near the ocean, most fish was processed first by drying, salting, pickling, or fermenting with a combination of salt and rice to become *narezushi*. Due to the difficulty of keeping fish fresh, probably only freshwater fish was consumed raw.

The species of fish mentioned above were luxury items, beyond the reach of nearly all commoners living at Heijōkyō.

43 WHAT KINDS OF VEGETABLES WERE CONSUMED?

Vegetables were either cultivated or gathered from the wild, often on hillsides.

Cultivated vegetables that still grace the tables of many homes in Japan include turnip, Japanese white radish, taro, and gourds. A less-known vegetable eaten in Heijōkyō was *chisha*, a kind of lettuce.

Wild greens picked in the mountains included Japanese bracken or *warabi* (*Allium macrostemon*), a plant from the onion family known as *nobiru*, a kind of yam called *yamaimo* (*Dioscorea japonica*), and tender shoots from the Japanese Angelica tree or *tara no me* (*Aralia elata*). Even today, some of these mountain-greens might be picked during the appropriate season and prepared with meals. Less familiar are the wild grasses collected during the Nara period, such as a kind of flowering plant known as *aoi* (*Malvaceae*) and a kind of buckwheat called *gishi gishi* (*Rumex*).

As opposed to eating the mountain vegetables freshly picked, culinary practices at Heijōkyō usually involved pickling the vegetables. This way, the preserved greens could be enjoyed all year long.

Mountain vegetables were only distributed to aristocrats and high-ranking officials by the state, so for everyone else there was no choice but to hunt around the sides of mountains to obtain their own tender edibles.

44 WHAT WERE FAVORITE FOODS OR SNACKS?

Aside from regular meals, a few other snack-like foods, namely confections and fruits, were consumed by the privileged minority as rather extravagant indulgences. The recipe for one confection mixes rice and flour together to form a sticky paste, then deep-frying small portions in oil to obtain a cracker or chip-like snack similar to what is known today as *senbei*.

Other confections might take sticky rice, soybeans, or red beans, and combine these in different proportions to make a kind of flattened sticky cake, or to create bite-sized sticky balls. Soybeans were also ground into a dry powder (*kinako*) and used as a flavorful coating for the small, sticky balls.

Fruits included pears, peaches, and persimmons. Also gathered from trees were chestnuts, walnuts, and nuts from the *shii* (*Castanopsis*) tree that look like pointed acorns. Persimmons were dried and stored along with the tree nuts.

As for sugary sweets, a kind of candy was made using rice and malt. Sugar and honey might be more familiar to us now, but these were rare, valuable commodities imported from abroad.

Although the confections and fruits mentioned above were generally out of reach for the general population, some varieties of fruit grew wild in the mountains and could be gathered.

45 WHAT KINDS OF
SEASONINGS WERE AVAILABLE?

Japanese cuisine is based on five essential seasonings summed up as "*sa shi su se so.*" This mnemonic device is a shortened version of these words "***satō shio su shō**yu mi**so***" or sugar, salt, vinegar, soy sauce, and *miso.*

During the time of Heijōkyō, a somewhat different but early prototype of the five seasonings was already in use. Salt was the most widely distributed, reaching all levels of the social strata. However, the quality of salt used by the privileged elite and the general population differed tremendously.

Nara-period soy sauce and *miso* were early prototypes of what are commonly available today, made using different base materials. The cost of vinegar and soy sauce was almost equivalent, as both were considered to be luxury items.

Sugar was an extreme luxury item, used as both a food seasoning and as medicine. Aristocrats and high-ranking officials qualified for limited sugar allotments but only on special occasions.

In addition to the five primary seasonings were other spices, such as mustard, *wasabi*, ginger, and a kind of Japanese pepper called *sanshō* (*Zanthoxylum*). The kind of pepper usually found in kitchens today was also available but rare. Other extreme luxury spices described in the literary record have since become obscure and are unknown.

At the present time, cooks in Japan use the seasonings mentioned above to create a diverse array of dishes and flavors. Yet at Heijōkyō, only a small minority of diners enjoyed a similar kind of food experience. The only seasoning most people at the capital ever tasted was salt.

46 WHAT DID SERVING BOWLS AND PLATES LOOK LIKE?

A specific type, size, and quantity of serving bowl and plate was permitted for each individual, depending on social position and rank. In other words, a quick glance at the type of dish that someone was using would immediately indicate their place in society.

A person of high rank mainly used metallic or lacquer bowls. Most commoners used dishes of either a low-fired, earthenware pottery called *hajiki*, or unglazed stoneware called *sueki*.

At the Heijō palace complex, the state provided meals to government officials. Because a vast amount of food was prepared and served, the shape and size of each plate or bowl was likely standardized to facilitate the stacking of vessels and streamline the serving process. You might have had a similar experience during lunchtime at school cafeterias, where standardized plates and trays are in continuous use.

47 WERE CHOPSTICKS USED?

Chopsticks were unearthed during archaeological surveys at Heijōkyō.

At the capital just before Heijōkyō, Fujiwarakyō, chopsticks have not been found and the material record indicates that spoons were used at Fujiwarakyō.

A great number of chopsticks were discovered at the site of the Heijō palace complex, likely used by officials during regular mealtimes and at special banquets. Stored inside Shōsōin repository were metallic chopsticks, apparently reserved for the Heavenly Sovereign or other high-ranking person.

The practice of using chopsticks seems to have been transmitted from the Korean peninsula during the Asuka period, initially becoming popular among the elite and gradually spreading to the general population.

48 DID A FAMILY EAT MEALS TOGETHER?

Detailed records were not kept concerning the daily habits of a typical commoner family, so how this sort of family ate meals is not entirely clear. However, surviving partial records describe the eating customs of courtiers.

Aristocrats usually held prominent government posts and, after finishing work during morning hours at the palace complex, often attended evening functions that included dinner. As for low-ranking officials, they usually worked overtime until late afternoon or nightfall. Although there were only two main meals per day at this time—once in the morning and once in the evening—a third, or in-between, meal known as *kanshoku* was provided to those engaged in manual labor and to officials working late into the night.

Judging from the daily routines of government officials, it seems unlikely that these families shared meals together. But in the case of commoners who did not receive prepared meals at the workplace, each family probably cooked and ate their meals together.

49 WERE COFFEE, TEA, AND ALCOHOLIC BEVERAGES SERVED?

During the time of Heijōkyō, coffee (sourced from Ethiopia in Africa) had not yet been introduced to Japan. Official envoys returning from Tang China, referred to as *kentōshi*, may have introduced tea to the capital, but no records detailing such exchange have been found. As for alcoholic beverages, the production and consumption of rice wine started much earlier than the founding of Heijōkyō. Mikinotsukasa, located inside the Heijō palace complex (see Map 3), was a government office managing the production of rice wine.

Rice wine at Heijōkyō was brewed by fermenting rice with a special mold called *kōji*. A similar method is still used to brew Japanese rice wine. Different varieties of rice wine were produced according to whether the lees, or residual rice pulp known as *sake kasu* left over after the fermentation process, were strained and removed to produce a clear liquid (*seishu*), or whether the lees remained in suspension to produce a cloudy rice wine (*nigori sake*). Aside from rice wine, a distilled alcoholic beverage called *shōchū* was also produced.

Rice wine and distilled alcoholic beverages were served during special rites, ceremonies, and banquets attended by aristocrats and high-ranking officials. Alcoholic potions were also used as medicine, perhaps like some of the cough syrups containing alcohol that we might buy at a pharmacy today. The general populace typically did not have access to rice wine and *shōchū* but instead, they could acquire the residual rice pulp or *sake kasu* to create a drink called *kasuyuzake* by mixing the rice pulp with hot water.

According to written records, drinking establishments at Heijōkyō, identified as *shushi*, seem to have served alcoholic beverages. Yet where the *shushi* were located within the capital and their exact nature are unknown.

PART SIX:
PARAMETERS OF HEIJŌKYŌ

* * *

50 HOW BIG WAS HEIJŌKYŌ, AND WHERE IS IT ON A MODERN MAP?

Heijōkyō measured about 4.2 kilometers from east to west, and about 4.8 kilometers from north to south. Including Gekyō on the east side, the total area of the capital was over twenty-four square kilometers. To provide a better sense of the size, about 513 Tokyo Dome athletic stadiums could fit inside Heijōkyō. The vertical and horizontal streets (*jōbō*) of Heijōkyō were aligned at ninety-degree angles to each other, forming a grid street pattern (see Map 2).

The Heijō palace complex occupied the center of the northern boundary of the capital. To locate the northern boundary of the capital on a modern street map, start at the north exit (*kitaguchi*) of the Kintetsu train line's Yamato Saidaiji station. Find the street originating near the north exit that runs east; the Heijōkyō northern boundary was established slightly north of this street.

To locate the southern border of the palace complex, find the monumental Suzaku Gate (see Figure 1). Serving as the gateway to the rest of the capital, Suzaku Gate opened onto the main thoroughfare called Suzaku Boulevard. Running north-south, Suzaku Boulevard intersected the capital. West of the boulevard was called Ukyo, and east of the boulevard was called Sakyō. At the southernmost end of Suzaku Boulevard was Rajō Gate, the gateway to the capital itself and part of the Heijōkyō southern boundary. The ruins of Rajō Gate today lie to the north of the JR train line's Kōriyama station, near the intersection of the Saho River and the road aligned in an east-west direction that borders the modern cities of Nara and Yamato Kōriyama.

Gekyō corresponds to the part of the capital located on the easternmost side of the capital, built in the area immediately east of the JR Nara train station. Its southern boundary lay just north of the JR Sakurai train line's Kyōbate station, and its northern boundary was the road aligned in an east-west direction which passes by the Tōdaiji Tegai

Gate (Tegaimon). The eastern boundary of Gekyō was the road aligned along a north-south direction and lies between Kōfukuji and the Nara National Museum. The district currently referred to as Naramachi generally corresponds to Gekyō.

Regarding the western boundary of the capital, it is speculated to have corresponded to the area lying east of the Kintetsu Ayame ike train station. Yet questions remain since this area is hilly, and the uneven terrain would not have been ideal for the construction of straight streets. If an opportunity to further excavate this area presents itself in the future, archaeologists could determine whether ancient buildings and roads had been laid out in accordance with the city grid, thereby confirming the western boundary of Heijōkyō.

51 HOW WAS HEIJŌKYŌ PORTRAYED IN EARLY DOCUMENTARY SOURCES?

A *Shoku nihongi* entry from 724.11.8 records a decree for courtiers of the fifth rank or higher, in addition to commoners who have the means to comply, to erect buildings at Heijōkyō with tiled roofs and exteriors painted red and white. Previously, with the exception of Buddhist temples, buildings were apparently rather drab in appearance, having rooftops shingled with wood board or thatch and taking on a weathered, perhaps even shabby, appearance over time.

Following this edict, brightly polychromed structures such as Suzaku Gate and Great Audience Hall were built, almost as if in competition with each other.

A few poems in *Manyōshū* reveal telling details concerning the nature of the capital and how it looked. Ono Oyu, a vice minister at Dazaifu, wrote a poem in remembrance of the capital describing his longing to return:

> The Imperial City of fairest Nara
> Glows now at the height of beauty,
> Like brilliant flowers in bloom![19]

Another poem collected in *Manyōshū* reflects the poet's yearning for the capital in springtime:

> In the Land where our Sovereign rules
> The Imperial City dwells
> Most dearly in my heart.

---

19 *Manyōshū* Volume 3, 328. The English translation was taken from Japanese Classics Translation Committee, eds., *1000 Poems from the Manyōshū: The Complete Nippon Gakujutsu Shinkokai Translation* (Mineola, New York: Dover Publications, 2005), poem 282 on page 97.

The waving wisterias are in full bloom;
Do they not remind you, my lord,
Of the Imperial City of Nara? [20]

According to a notation in *Manyōshū*, Ōtomo Yotsuna, a vice-minister at the office overseeing the management of frontier troops, likely addressed this poem to the Governor General of Dazaifu, Ōtomo Tabito.

These poems conjure up an image of Heijōkyō as a beautiful, dazzling city of flowers and brilliantly colored buildings.

---

20 *Manyōshū* Volume 3, 329-330. The English translation was taken from Japanese Classics Translation Committee, eds., *1000 Poems from the Manyōshū: The Complete Nippon Gakujutsu Shinkokai Translation* (Mineola, New York: Dover Publications, 2005), poems 558-559 on pages 184-185.

52 Aside from serving as a thoroughfare, was Suzaku Boulevard used in other ways?

Suzaku Boulevard was about seventy-five meters wide as confirmed through archaeological survey. As a means of comparison, since the average automobile measures less than three meters, Suzaku Boulevard could have been divided into a twenty-five lane road. Quite spacious, was it not?

You might wonder why such a wide road was necessary. Rajō Gate on the southern end of Suzaku Boulevard functioned as the gateway to the capital, and when foreign envoys came to visit Heijōkyō an elaborate welcome ceremony was staged in front of Rajō Gate. No other gate at Heijōkyō was as large as Rajō Gate. Passing through Rajō Gate, envoys entered Heijōkyō and proceeded north on Suzaku Boulevard for about 3.7 kilometers to the main entrance to the palace complex, Suzaku Gate. The procession along Suzaku Boulevard was staged as a majestic spectacle. In this fashion, the main artery in the capital did not serve only as a street but functioned as a space to perform important state rituals and ceremonies. To fulfill this second role, Suzaku Boulevard was planned as a very wide street.

Earthen walls were erected on both sides of Suzaku Boulevard, and as Ōtomo Yakamochi wistfully recalled in his poem appearing in *Manyōshū* (Volume 19, 4142) willow trees were planted along the boulevard. Perhaps most important, Suzaku Boulevard was carefully planned to gradually increase in altitude; in other words, after visitors entered Rajō Gate and started to approach Suzaku Gate from the south, the perspective of seeing the palace complex loom slightly higher in the distance served to create an impression of a soaring and perhaps imposing palace. Crafting this image of a stately royal capital was no small task.

53 WHO CLEANED THE STREETS?

A government office, Kyōshiki, was responsible for maintaining the streets and bridges at Heijōkyō.

A stream of water continuously flowed through the gutters built along both sides of a street. If the gutters were to ever get blocked then raw sewage would overflow, creating an environmental hazard. To prevent such a disaster, the government office employed *shichō* who maintained and repaired the gutters before they became blocked.

As for routine street-cleaning, this task fell upon residents of homes lining the streets. Kyōshiki supervised the households, ensuring that residents were diligently performing their duties.

Keeping the streets clean was not only critical to maintaining a sanitary environment but also served to create and maintain an image of a sacred capital inhabited by the Heavenly Sovereign—a place that appeared pristine, unpolluted, and orderly to visitors coming from distant regions. Yet there remains the possibility that because the area within the capital was so large, Kyōshiki was unable to adequately monitor every street. Perhaps for this reason, archaeologists have unearthed street gutters that had, in fact, become repeatedly blocked and needed to be dug out.

54 WHAT WAS THE LARGEST BUILDING AT HEIJŌKYŌ?

The largest building was the Tōdaiji Golden Hall (also known as Daibutsuden), and the current structure is still famous as the world's largest wooden building. Built in the Edo period during a massive rebuilding campaign, the present Daibutsuden is not as big as the original building; the Nara-period Daibutsuden was 1.5 times wider than the current structure, and certainly must have been the largest building at the time. The current Daibutsuden measures fifty-seven meters in width and forty-nine meters in height.

To be precise, however, Tōdaiji did not lie within Heijōkyō. Tōdaiji was built just outside the eastern border of Gekyō. Accordingly, the largest building at Heijōkyō would likely have been Great Audience Hall inside the Heijō palace complex. Great Audience Hall is believed to have measured forty-four meters in width and twenty-nine meters in height.

As for the tallest structure, the East Pagoda and West Pagoda at Daianji would have risen higher than any other building at the capital. Each seven-story pagoda is speculated to have measured about seventy meters in height. A team of archaeologists administered by Nara city, Narashi kyōiku iinkai, excavated the foundation of a Daianji pagoda and discovered the *fūtaku* or windbell that hung from the eaves. The scale of the windbell is of such great magnitude that it will astonish just about anyone.

Turning our attention back now to Tōdaiji, according to a record from the document *Tōdaiji yōroku* the Tōdaiji seven-story East Pagoda and West Pagoda measured about one hundred meters in height, standing even taller than the Daianji twin pagodas.[21]

---

21 First compiled in 1106, *Tōdaiji yōroku* in ten volumes contains records of various aspects relating to Tōdaiji, including its operation and history.

55 DO ANY OF THE HEIJŌ PALACE BUILDINGS REMAIN EXTANT?

Very few Heijō palace complex structures dating to the Nara period survive today. Most buildings were dismantled and transferred further north to the Nagaoka palace complex at Nagaokakyō, which was briefly established as the next capital.[22]

One surviving example of palace architecture dating to the Nara period is the Lecture Hall of the Buddhist temple Tōshōdaiji (see no.18 in Map 2), where a palace building was reused to become a temple building. Specifically, the Tōshōdaiji Lecture Hall initially functioned as part of the Chōshūden or State Assembly Halls located at the Heijō palace complex. This Assembly Hall was dismantled, transferred to Tōshōdaiji, and refashioned in the style of a Buddhist temple building. A ninth-century history of Tōshōdaiji, *Shōdaiji konryū engi*, relates this series of events.

Tōshōdaiji was founded in 759 by the eminent Chinese monk Ganjin (Ch. Jianzhen), who was asked to come to Heijō from Tang. In order to swiftly accommodate the needs of Ganjin after his long-awaited arrival to Heijōkyō, an Assembly Hall from the palace complex was moved to Tōshōdaiji.

When the Tōshōdaiji Lecture Hall was restored during the modern period, structural details revealed that the initial palace building had faced west; in other words, the entrance to the Assembly Hall was located on the west side. As part of a group of buildings at the palace complex facing an open courtyard, a west-facing building would have been situated on the east side of the courtyard. Although somewhat reconfigured, the Tōshōdaiji Lecture Hall offers us a rare glimpse of architecture from the Heijō palace complex.

---

22 Nagaokakyō served as the capital between 784 and 794. In 794 the capital was again transferred further north to Heiankyō in what is now Kyoto. For an in-depth monograph on the Nagaoka capital, see *Nagaoka: Japan's Forgotten Capital* by Ellen Van Goethem (Leiden: Brill, 2008).

56 Were gardens and parks constructed at Heijōkyō?

Archaeologists have unearthed evidence of ancient gardens at numerous sites within Heijōkyō. Ruins of gardens were found at residential quarters of the palace, government offices, temples, and aristocratic residences. An ancient garden that is famous today was unearthed at Tōin or East Palace, located on the east side of the Heijō palace complex. Another garden, Shōrin'en, was a special garden built exclusively for the Heavenly Sovereign on the north side of the palace complex. At Shōrin'en, a preexisting mounded tomb was reused to create the garden; the moat surrounding the tomb was altered to form a pond, and the mound was made to look like a miniature island rising up out of the lake.

Gardens during this period were mainly used as places for conducting rites or holding banquets. Basic features of the garden later developed into what are now identified as traditional Japanese gardens.

Traces from the past were used as guides to completely restore two ruined gardens that are now open to the public. The East Palace garden (see Figure 5) or Tōin teien, lies inside the Heijō palace complex while the other lies outside the complex. This second garden is known by the street address at Heijōkyō, or Heijōkyō sakyō sanjō nibō, and is located to the south of the large mall Itō Yōkadō Nara (Sanjō ōji in Nara city). A visit to these gardens will introduce you to the sights and sounds enjoyed by Heijōkyō aristocrats.

57 DID CANALS FLOW THROUGH HEIJŌKYŌ?

East Marketplace (Higashi no ichi) was located at Heijōkyō sakyō hachijō sanbō near present-day Karamomo chō and Higashi kujō chō in Nara city (see no.9 in Map 2). When this area was excavated, a dry riverbed about ten meters in width and 1.4 meters in depth was discovered to the east of East Marketplace. This river once served as a canal at Heijōkyō named Higashi horikawa.

West Marketplace (Nishi no ichi) was situated at Heijōkyō ukyō hachijō nibō near present-day Kujō chō in Yamato Kōriyama city (see no.10 in Map 2). Akishino River still winds around the east side of the West Marketplace ruins. This river was probably redirected to form a canal referred to as Nishi horikawa.

In this fashion, the canals flowing adjacent to East and West Marketplace served as critical waterways and were used to transport goods. Additionally, Saho River, flowing on the east side of the capital, probably functioned as another important waterway. Careful examination of all rivers flowing through Heijōkyō reveals several that were aligned in a north-south or east-west direction generally corresponding with the grid street system. This indicates that during the construction of the capital, the natural course of many rivers and streams were likely altered to form shipping canals.

58 HOW MANY BRIDGES WERE BUILT OVER THE WATERWAYS AT HEIJŌKYŌ?

The two main waterways flowing through the center of Heijōkyō were Akishino River on the west side (Ukyō) and Saho River on the east side (Sakyō). Tributary streams fed both rivers. Higashi horikawa, a canal and gutter used to transport goods as well as sewage, was constructed at Sakyō by digging out earth to form a channel, while Akishino River, flowing through Ukyō, was renamed Nishi horikawa.

The maximum width of the rivers was more than ten meters, so bridges were likely built over canals at street crossings. Ruins of wooden bridge supports were unearthed at several sites, yet the total number of bridges that once existed at Heijōkyō remains unconfirmed.

While the exact number of bridges at the capital is unclear, we do know there were many. Bridges were critical to sustaining the flow of traffic within the capital, and contemporary written documents inform us that government agencies were in charge of maintaining these bridges.

PART SEVEN:
INTERNATIONAL
METROPOLIS, HEIJŌKYŌ

* * *

59 FOREIGN EMISSARIES ARRIVED FROM WHICH COUNTRIES?

The most frequent visitors to Heijōkyō came from Unified Silla on the Korean peninsula. Next were visitors from Parhae, located at the northern region of the Korean peninsula and the northeastern region of China (see Map 1). Unified Silla and Parhae also participated in diplomatic exchange with each other.

Travelers from Tang (China) also arrived at Heijōkyō. One of the most famous might be Ganjin, mentioned earlier in Question 55. Other monks at Heijōkyō originated from Tenjiku (India) and Rinyū (Vietnam).

In a somewhat different context, inhabiting what is now northeastern Japan and southern Kyūshū were groups of people who refused to submit to the authority of the central government located at Heijōkyō. Proof of their eventual submission was forcibly displayed by bringing such individuals to Heijōkyō and having them participate in various official rites and ceremonies.

60 Where did foreign visitors reside during their stay?

Foreign visitors to Japan consisted of diplomatic envoys, monastic clergy, and merchants. Most visitors to Heijōkyō, however, were envoys and clergy. Foreign merchants conducted business at Tsukushi no murotsumi (a forerunner to Kōrokan), a government facility intended to foster foreign exchange. The ruins of this structure were unearthed at the Heiwadai kyūjō site in Fukuoka city, Fukuoka prefecture, Kyūshū.

While monastic clergy arriving from overseas stayed at Buddhist temples, no records describe where envoys lodged at Heijōkyō. Envoys entering the capital would first convey their greetings to the Heavenly Sovereign at the Heijō palace complex and then exchange gifts and letters sent from their monarch or emperor. A banquet would follow, and afterwards the official guests were probably escorted to some kind of special facility. In a later example, Kōrokan at the Heian capital served as a place for both lodging and entertaining foreign guests, so a similar kind of facility likely existed at the Heijō capital as well.

Prior to entering the capital, protocols dictated that foreign envoys pass through a series of checkpoints. At the first point of entry, Tsukushi no murotsumi, envoys were asked the reason for their visit, and their belongings were inspected. If there were no problems the envoys boarded a ship that traveled across the Seto Inland Sea and headed for what is now Osaka. Upon reaching the port known as Naniwa no tsu—near Osaka castle today—passengers disembarked and were entertained at a nearby reception hall or inn. Afterwards, the envoys proceeded on to Heijōkyō. This route was predominantly taken by Unified Silla envoys.

As for Parhae envoys, their boats docked along the coastline of the Sea of Japan, or present-day prefectures of Hyōgo, Fukui, Ishikawa, Niigata, and Shimane. After arriving on the coast, Parhae envoys sojourned in the area for two to three months before they were escorted to Heijōkyō on an overland route. However, if the letter from the Parhae sovereign was insulting or offensive in any way, the envoys would not be invited to Heijōkyō but sent back to Parhae. The envoys would also be instructed to enter Japan through the official gateway at Tsukushi (Fukuoka city) on their next visit.

61 WHAT WAS THE PURPOSE OF A FOREIGN ENVOY'S VISIT?

Foreign envoys played a crucial role in maintaining good relations between neighboring kingdoms and helped negotiate resolutions to avoid conflicts and wars. Envoys to Japan usually brought greetings and delivered gifts to the Heavenly Sovereign and to powerful courtiers. In return, the Heavenly Sovereign entertained the envoys and distributed gifts.

On the first day of the first month of the new year, envoys attended court at Heijōkyō and sent felicitations for the new year to the Heavenly Sovereign. They also participated in a special ceremony involving the shooting of arrows. Aside from new year ceremonies, envoys attended celebrations ushering in the reign of a new Heavenly Sovereign. The reasons behind a foreign envoy's visit shifted according to power relationships between the kingdoms.

Some of the envoys brought over a diverse array of goods and engaged in commerce. Stored at Shōsōin repository are documents of trade with Unified Silla representatives during the Nara period. Powerful aristocrats at Heijōkyō competed to purchase highly coveted imports from Unified Silla: incense, medicines, paints, mirrors, metallic tableware, carpets, and honey.

62 HOW DID LOCAL OFFICIALS COMMUNICATE WITH THEIR GUESTS FROM ABROAD?

Translators accompanied official missions coming from abroad, so envoys communicated with their hosts at Heijōkyō through their translators. A second set of interpreters attended the hosts, allowing for fluent two-way exchanges.

Aside from foreign envoys, Buddhist monks originating from Tang (China), Tenjiku (India), Rinyū (Vietnam), Hashi, Kokoku, and Konron also came to Heijōkyō. Since these monks had most likely lived and studied at China prior to arriving at Heijōkyō, they would have been fluent in Chinese. The monks likely spoke Chinese to an interpreter or transcribed Chinese characters in order to communicate.

63 WHAT KINDS OF GIFTS WERE GIVEN?

The type and quantity of gifts distributed to visiting foreign envoys depended on the status of the receiver. A list of appropriate gifts for specific recipients appears in a book of laws and regulations compiled in the tenth century, *Engishiki*.

Gifts to the Tang Emperor included silver, woven silk textiles, silk floss, cloth, cotton, precious stones, flint, and camellia oil. Silk products, minerals, and oils were submitted as tax payments to Heijōkyō from all over Japan, and were more like raw materials than finished products. Because superbly exquisite and rare objects from around the world were brought to Tang, the Emperor may have preferred to receive raw materials of high quality from Japan as opposed to receiving finished products whose level of craftsmanship was not particularly high.

Gifts to the Unified Silla Monarch and the Parhae Monarch also included silk products and cloth, but the quantity was about one-tenth of what was provided to the Tang Emperor.

64 What was the selection process for envoys dispatched from Japan to China?

Kentōshi, official envoys sent to Tang China, seem to have been dispatched on eighteen separate missions, but only fifteen missions actually crossed the seas.

Each mission involved between one hundred and two hundred fifty people who boarded four boats heading to China (see Figure 6). In addition to envoys, missions included record keepers, craftsmen, sailors, and students going to study secular or religious subjects abroad. Since the purpose of sending *kentōshi* was to learn more about Tang culture, a mission might also include doctors, painters, and musicians. *Kentōshi* primarily sought to learn and import advanced new methods of governance, cultural and religious practices, and technologies from China.

As for the *kentōshi* selection process, while this is not entirely clear it seems that highly cultured, learned officials and monastic clergy were generally dispatched. Famous examples are the poet-courtier Yamanoue Okura, the scholar-courtier Kibi Makibi, and the monk Genbō from the Nara period, or the monks Saichō and Kūkai from the Heian period.

Before departing for China, the Great Envoy (*taishi*) received a ceremonial sword (*settō*) from the Heavenly Sovereign, symbolizing the authority accorded to the holder of the sword. One courtier named Saeki Imaemishi, who had actively supported the construction of Tōdaiji and Saidaiji, was appointed as Great Envoy to Tang in 774.6. However, after arriving at present-day Okayama prefecture he requested a delay of one year before crossing to Tang. Saeki then returned home and promptly returned the ceremonial sword.

The following year, Saeki once again received the ceremonial sword and was expected to set sail for China. This time, however, after reaching Rajō Gate at Heijōkyō he complained of illness and, in the end, did not go to Tang. Making the long journey across the seas to Tang was treacherous and fraught with mortal dangers, so it is not too surprising that Saeki wanted to avoid taking such risks.

PART EIGHT:
FINANCE AND MARKETS

* * *

65 WHAT KINDS OF TAXES WERE LEVIED?

Taxes during the Nara period consisted of *so, yō, chō,* and *zōyō*.

So were taxes based on rice field harvests, levied at about 3 to 5 percent per unit of rice field. Since rice field allotments for each Heijōkyō resident was located outside the capital, they commuted to cultivate their fields.

Yō was generally the payment of rice, textiles, or special regional products as substitutes for tribute in labor by those living in the provinces. People residing at Heijōkyō or at a neighboring province were exempted from this tax.

Chō was the payment of textiles, seafood, or other regional delicacies. This tax requirement was reduced to about half for Heijōkyō residents, who often submitted payment in cash instead of goods.

Zōyō was a tax paid in manual labor and might involve repair work on bridges or buildings. Sixty working days per year were required.

While it might appear that living at the capital secured tax exemptions and preferential treatment, residents were often compelled to provide labor in addition to their tax requirements—life was anything but easy for Heijōkyō residents.

66 WHEN PEOPLE FROM DISTANT PROVINCES JOURNEYED TO THE CAPITAL TO PAY THEIR TAXES, WHERE DID THEY STAY?

A person who transported or shipped taxes from the periphery to the capital was called an *unkyakufu*, and each province was responsible for managing their own shippers. A province was required to pay a certain amount in taxes to the central government, and if the goods could not be procured within the province then the items needed to be purchased at the Heijōkyō East or West Marketplace. To assist with this process, it seems that each province established an administrative or storage facility near a marketplace. Lodging for shippers was probably located at each administrative facility as well.

The Sagami province (present-day Kanagawa prefecture) administrative facility was established near East Marketplace, at Heijōkyō sakyō hachijō sanbō (present-day Karamomo chō and Higashi kujō chō in Nara city). According to recent archaeological findings, the facility for Harima province (present-day Hyōgo prefecture) is believed to have been established near Heijōkyō sakyō gojō shibō.

67 WHAT KIND OF CURRENCY WAS IN CIRCULATION?

A coin often referred to as Wadō kaichin was first issued around the time that Heijōkyō was established. Each of the four characters in the name appears on a coin, but the characters themselves are actually simplified versions of four characters: *wa* is the same character on both the coin and full inscription, *dō* on the coin has been truncated from the character for "bronze," *kai* is unchanged, and *chin* on the coin takes only the top section of the character for "treasure." Since the character for "treasure" is actually pronounced *hō* in Japanese, the coin may have been called Wadō kaihō when it was in circulation. Initially, both a silver and copper version of this coin was in use, but after 709.8 the silver coin fell out of use.

Following Wadō kaihō another coin, Mannen tsūhō, was issued in 760.3. Next, Jingō kaihō was minted between 765 and 796. The government office Chūsenshi minted the coins, and subsidiary offices of Chūsenshi were located at the provinces of Kawachi (Osaka prefecture), Yamashiro (Kyoto prefecture), and Nagato (Yamaguchi prefecture).

While copper coins were most prevalent, also in circulation were a limited number of gold and silver coins. For example, around the time when Mannen tsūhō was in active use, the silver coin was called Taihei genpō and the gold coin Kaiki shōhō. The silver coin was worth ten times as much as a copper, and a gold coin was worth one hundred times as much as a copper.

Using the cost of rice as a gauge to understand the value of currency, we can observe that inflation was severe: in the year 751, one unit of rice (*itto*) was equivalent to 50 *mon*; thirteen years later or in 764, one unit of rice cost 300 *mon*; seven years later or in 771, one unit of rice cost 650 *mon*.

According to contemporary records, coins were used to pay taxes, wages to manual laborers, and fees for renting a cart. Coins were also collected to support social and religious causes. One wooden document notes the donation of 200 *mon* towards the construction of the monumental Vairocana Buddha at Tōdaiji. This donation came from a fundraising group situated at a government office, Moitori no tsukasa. Coworkers at this office might have been compelled to contribute a small amount of money towards a specific, and presumably worthy, cause.

68 WHERE COULD RESIDENTS BUY GROCERIES AND DAILY LIVING ESSENTIALS?

Shops at Heijōkyō were located at East Marketplace and West Marketplace, the former located at Heijōkyō sakyō hachijō sanbō and the latter at Heijōkyō ukyō hachijō nibō. A government office, Ichi no tsukasa, regulated the markets. Since goods shipped in from all over Japan were available for purchase at the state markets, the market scene must have been quite lively.

A wide variety of goods were sold at the shops: grains, fresh produce, seafood, textiles, and other daily essentials. Representatives from government offices and Buddhist temples came to purchase necessary supplies or sell items at their own storefronts. Some aristocratic households, such as Prince Nagaya, employed craftspeople who specialized in producing goods both for use within the household and for sale at market. That is, we know the Nagayaō household operated a shop at the marketplace according to records inscribed on wooden documents.

Heijōkyō residents could also purchase goods at other shops located outside the capital.

69 How many shops engaged in business at Heijōkyō East Marketplace and West Marketplace?

This is a good question. At the present time, we have no means to find out the precise answer. However, the Heian-period document *Engishiki* includes a list of shops and might shed some light on this issue.

Shops at the Heian capital sold various items. You could find textiles such as silk, cotton, woven fabric, and brocades. Shops sold the kind of items you might find at your corner drugstore, such as combs, needles, writing brushes, ink, medicines, and incense. Weapons such as arrows and swords were also available for purchase, as were grocery items like bowls and plates, oils, salt, rice, fresh produce, and seafood. Perhaps unusual for today would be the shops selling cows and horses. While the exact number of shops in business at Heiankyō is unknown, we know there were many diverse establishments; a similar situation likely prevailed at Heijōkyō as well.

Could anyone offer goods for sale at the marketplace? Genshiryō, a set of laws regulating market activities, does not list specific restrictions on who could open a shop at East Marketplace or West Marketplace. However, Ichi no tsukasa, the government office regulating the markets, strictly enforced a set of marketplace rules. For instance, items for sale needed to be listed on a signboard, selling inferior quality goods was prohibited, and prices were closely monitored by Ichi no tsukasa.

Not only individuals set up and operated shops. Provincial government officials charged with submitting taxes to the central government might open a storefront to raise funds necessary to procure essential provisions or goods, perhaps through barter or exchange.

Shops were open between noon and sunset, with segregation between women and men.

PART NINE:
Anxieties at Heijōkyō

* * *

70 WHAT WERE SOURCES OF TROUBLE?

Unsanitary conditions at the capital gave rise to outbreaks of epidemics. Aside from worrying about disease, other troubles plaguing Heijōkyō residents included heavy tax burdens and harsh working conditions when fulfilling mandatory physical labor requirements.

Densely populated Heijōkyō is considered to be among the first cities in Japan. In such a place residents had no choice but to interact with many other people, regardless of whether they wished to or not. In the case of a low-ranking government official, he was required to work long hours on a daily basis, all the while subjected to relentless criticisms by a rather despicable superior. Socializing with colleagues was another difficult task, as complicated personal relationships led to considerable anxiety. Under such conditions, psychological stress probably accumulated in a manner that was previously unimaginable.

Archaeologists discovered various objects that apparently functioned to rid the body of *kegare* or impurities (see Question 96), as treatment for physical and psychological ailments. For example, small wooden boards shaped like a human body (*katashiro*) were unearthed. Also found were small clay bowls with a person's face depicted on the exterior surface in black ink. Someone believed to be afflicted by *kegare* attempted to rid their body of impurities by transferring the toxic sources of their physical and psychological ailments onto one of these effigy-like objects, and then floated the object down a river, stream, or gutter.

Do we have a similar kind of practice during the twenty-first century?

71 DID NATURAL DISASTERS OCCUR?

According to written records, Heijōkyō was stricken by droughts, floods, devastating storms, and earthquakes.

Few written records describe flood damage, but roadside gutters blocked with waste and garbage probably flooded regularly following heavy rains. Because the regular disposal of waste products into gutters already impeded the flow of water at any given time, a sudden deluge of water or muddy debris into the gutters immediately led to a disastrous situation.

Also, given the state of severe deforestation at the mountains surrounding Heijōkyō—the trees were extracted and used as lumber or were burned as fuel—heavy rains likely caused streams of muddy debris to cascade down the treeless mountainsides and into the capital. A substantial number of landslides are speculated to have occurred, but perhaps the high frequency and common occurrence of municipal flooding made it unworthy of noting in official records.

After a landslide, the debris was cleared from the gutters to enable the flow of water again. In other words, by this period an emergency response system was already in place to combat natural disasters—a revelation that was somewhat unexpected and surprising when first realized by archaeologists.

72 WAS FIRE A MAJOR CONCERN?

When a large population of people lives in close proximity, fires occur frequently. Nearly half of the capital at Kyoto, Heiankyō, was known to have burned down at one time or other.

Even though approximately 100,000 people lived at Heijōkyō, references to fire in the written records are almost nonexistent. An exception is a fire recorded on 764.8.3 at a warehouse belonging to the Ministry of Finance.

Buildings situated at the palace complex and the Buddhist temples used fire-repellant tiles on the roof, but nearly all other structures in the capital were roofed with wood board or thatch, which would burn instantly in the event of a fire. While conditions were ripe for major fires to sweep through Heijōkyō, there are no written records that describe such an event. The archaeological record confirms this notion as few buildings show evidence of incineration during the time of Heijōkyō. Could it be possible that an effective system of fire prevention had been established? To be certain, government institutions at the time wielded considerable authority, so perhaps this was the case.

73 WHAT KINDS OF DISEASES AND EPIDEMICS WERE THERE?

You might have heard news reports over the past few years about new strains of influenza virus spreading from one country to another. During the Nara period, this happened too.

According to an entry recorded in *Shoku nihongi* and dated 735.8.12, news circulated of many people dying of disease at Dazaifu (Kyūshū). In an entry dated 735.8.23, Dazaifu administrators submitted an official request asking for tax exemptions of *chō* (regional products) because farmers throughout the region were dying from an epidemic. This was none other than the deadly smallpox outbreak.

The epidemic was briefly contained, but a second wave followed as indicated by an entry dated 737.4.19. Again farmers were dying throughout Kyūshū. The central government at Heijōkyō responded by instructing provincial administrators to send prayers to the deities, to assist poor and needy families, and to distribute medicine to the sick. In an entry dated 737.6.1, the government suspended court at Heijōkyō since many officials were sickened by the epidemic. This entry indicates that about a month after the second smallpox outbreak started at Kyūshū, the disease had spread to Heijōkyō. As a measure to contain the spread of smallpox, the Council of State (Daijōkan) disseminated specific instructions to each province on how to contain and remedy the disease.

Other entries dating to this period in *Shoku nihongi* list the deaths of a surprisingly large number of courtiers who succumbed to smallpox. Four sons of Fujiwara Fuhito—Muchimaro, Fukisaki, Umakai, and Maro—died in succession, highlighting the sense that no matter how much political and economic power a family might possess, no one was immune to the disease.

74 WHAT SORT OF MEDICINE WAS AVAILABLE?

Advances in medicine have given us many remedies as well as the means to examine causes of sickness. What was it like for Heijōkyō residents?

The practice of medicine during the Nara period was limited to basic and simple treatments. A person employed at the Office of Scripture Transcription submitted a written excuse to explain his absence, claiming that he was taking medicine to stop diarrhea. One such medicine might have been *manbyō kō* or "remedy for all (literally, ten-thousand) kinds of disease." Clay vessels were found with *manbyō kō* inscribed on the surface in black ink.

Medicine was based on traditional Chinese remedies, often consisting of herbs, grasses, roots, and other materials. Medicinal grasses might be immersed in rice wine to serve as a kind of tonic. According to a set of laws pertaining to medical treatment, Ishitsuryō, medical students at the Bureau of Medicine (Tenyakuryō) were required to study the texts *Honsō*. The traditional Chinese medicines described in *Honsō* were likely prepared and dispensed at Heijōkyō.

The Office of Remedies cultivated medicinal plants and also received shipments from other provinces as indicated by inscribed wooden strips used as shipping labels. Another medical institution, Seyakuin, was established in 730.4 and functioned like a hospital. Seyakuin provided acupuncture and massage treatments, in addition to Chinese medicine.

During periods of massive disease outbreaks, intensive prayers made to both Buddhist and local deities (*kami*) usually accompanied medical treatments.

75 HOW WAS GARBAGE DISPOSED?

Prior to the establishment of a large city like Heijōkyō, garbage was dumped into nearby rivers, ravines, or other low-lying areas. The amount of garbage was limited and mostly decomposed relatively easily.

However, with the advent of such densely populated cities like Heijōkyō, an inordinate amount of garbage was generated. In addition, residences at the capital were surrounded by streets on all four sides so disposing trash was no longer an easy task. Since there was no organized trash collection service for the community, residents would either dig a hole within their residential plot and bury their garbage or throw it into the gutters running alongside the streets.

These methods probably worked better than they would today since the amount of hazardous waste was significantly less, and most of the garbage could decompose on its own.

76 WERE THERE ENVIRONMENTAL PROBLEMS AND POLLUTION?

Many workshops lined the periphery of East Marketplace and West Marketplace, and disposed their waste products in the nearby canals. Leather-working workshops dumped large quantities of horse and cattle bones into the canals, which were later unearthed by archaeologists.

Since the entire population at the capital eliminated their waste in this manner, environmental conditions at the southern end of Heijōkyō would have become progressively worse as more and more garbage accumulated downstream. The smell must have been horrible.

Such unsanitary conditions would have accelerated the spread of diseases such as smallpox, resulting in high numbers of fatalities. This image of Heijōkyō contrasts sharply with the fond memory of the city in bloom as described by Ono Oyu in a *Manyōshū* poem (see Question 51).

77 WAS THERE FEAR OF INVASION BY ENEMIES?

With the exception of the area near Rajō Gate, the southern and main entrance to Heijōkyō, high walls were not built around the perimeter of the capital. That is, the capital was not a walled city and stood defenseless from intruders in this sense. Rice fields likely dotted the landscape outside the capital. The lack of a defensive wall around the perimeter of the capital is a distinctive characteristic of the Japanese capital and a major departure from the Tang capital of Chang'an.

The image of the capital unfortified by high walls might give you an impression of a pastoral and peaceful city, but Heijōkyō was in fact heavily guarded. The *hyōe* and *eji* troops (see Question 16), consisting of several thousand men at its peak, protected and policed the capital. In the event of a revolt or other disturbance, the troops assembled quickly. In actuality, Heijōkyō was like a kind of police state.

So despite being without a defensive wall around the capital, Heijōkyō seems to have been adequately secured by other defensive mechanisms. It can be assumed that Heijōkyō was always on guard against potential threats.

PART TEN:
EDUCATION AND
KNOWLEDGE IN THE CAPITAL

* * *

78 WERE SCHOOLS ESTABLISHED?

Attendance at elementary and junior high school is part of compulsory education in Japan today, but children living at Heijōkyō did not attend school. However, there were schools that trained students to become government officials.

Affiliated with the Ministry of Personal Affairs, Civil Services, and Ceremonies (Shikibushō) was the Bureau of Higher Education (Daigakuryō). Professors taught more than four hundred students at Daigakuryō, a government institution that corresponds roughly to our universities and colleges. Entering students were between the ages of thirteen and sixteen. Although any student can apply for and enter college in modern Japan, during the Nara period this was an exclusive privilege reserved for the children of courtiers and for descendants of recent immigrants (*toraijin*) who might already possess strong foreign language skills due to their family background.

Students at Daigakuryō read classical Chinese texts, practiced calligraphy, and perfected their arithmetic. Rules pertaining to student conduct were likely rigorous and difficult examinations were part of the curriculum as well.

Since enrollment at Daigakuryō was predominantly limited to aristocratic families, entrance to the college was not particularly competitive. Further, government positions were largely hereditary in nature; the child of a courtier was automatically given a government job in accordance with the rank and position of the parent. With their jobs already guaranteed, relatively few children of courtiers sought to attend Daigakuryō.

79 HOW DID PEOPLE LEARN TO WRITE?

A Chinese poem with the translated title *Thousand Character Classic* (J. *Senjimon*, Ch. *Qianziwen*) was used as a basic text to teach the one thousand characters appearing in the poem. In certain respects, this poem functioned like the alphabet song that children now sing to learn their ABCs. At Daigakuryō the classical Chinese texts known as *Analects* or *Analects of Confucius* (J. *Rongo*, Ch. *Lunyu*) were also used to practice writing skills.

Because paper was a highly valued and limited commodity, students practiced writing on rectangular strips of wood. A student would write on the *mokkan* surface with black ink and then shave off the top layer of wood to expose a clean, new surface. Reading and writing were the foremost duty of any official, and *mokkan* used to practice writing were unearthed throughout Heijōkyō.

As archaeologists sifted through the discarded *mokkan*, some were written by a person possessing exquisite penmanship while others compelled modern readers to wonder if the author were indeed literate and knew what the characters meant. Taken as a whole, the material evidence suggests that many people would simply pick up a piece of wood whenever they had free time and practiced writing over and over—possibly in anticipation of getting ahead in the world as a government official.

After learning Chinese characters, the next step was learning to write sentences. *Mokkan* suggestive of this kind of activity—such as copying sections of legal codes, official documents, and Chinese classical texts—have also been found at Heijōkyō.

80 WERE THERE LIBRARIES?

Literary works at Heijōkyō were primarily Chinese classics. Affiliated with the Ministry of Central Affairs (Nakatsukasashō) was the Bureau of Books and Drawings (Zushoryō), a government office charged with overseeing the storage and reproduction of books and drawings. A similar institution today would be the Diet Library in Japan or the Library of Congress in the United States.

Because Zushoryō was not open to the general public, it was not like the public libraries that might be familiar to you now. The first library of this sort in Japan was established by Isonokami Yakatsugu during the Nara period. The name of the structure housing the library was Untei. A description of Untei in a *Shoku nihongi* entry dating to 781.6 relates the conversion of a private residence into a Buddhist temple with one section transformed into Untei. Housed inside the library was a collection of books mostly unrelated to Buddhist scriptures. Upon request a person would be granted entry to browse and study the books. The ruins of Untei are believed to lie in the vicinity of a private high school in Nara city, Ichijō kōkō, and a memorial pillar currently stands at the site.

The total number of books in Japan at this time is unknown but might be comparable to a figure determined about a century later. At the end of the ninth century the Heavenly Sovereign issued an order to list every book in Japan, resulting in *Nihonkoku kenzaisho mokuroku*, which accounted for 16,790 volumes. Although it is difficult to gauge the total number of books during the Nara period, the figure must have been quite substantial.

81 HOW ADVANCED WAS THEIR MATH?

Streets intersected at ninety-degree angles at Heijōkyō along north-south and east-west axes and were set apart at regular intervals. This indicates that city planners were able to survey and lay out streets with a high degree of accuracy and regularity. Surveying land requires specialized skills. According to classical Chinese texts, placing an upright pole on flat ground and then carefully reading the shadows cast by the sun at specific times enables surveyors to mark off a straight, east-west line. Next, a line that intersects at ninety degrees, or a north-south line, could be determined.

Dividing and subdividing land into regular wards and residential plots—whether at a scale of one half, one fourth, or one eighth—indicates the ability to add, subtract, multiply, and divide.

An ancient Chinese text on arithmetic also states the special properties distinctive to a right triangle, specifically the relationship between the two shorter sides and the hypotenuse 3:4:5 (otherwise known as the Pythagorean theorem, $3^2+4^2=5^2$). This theorem may have been used to help plan the street grid at Heijōkyō.

82 WERE ASTRONOMICAL OBSERVATIONS MADE?

Nihon shoki contains records of various celestial phenomena such as phases of the moon, lunar and solar eclipses, and appearances of comets. It was the responsibility of the Divination Bureau at the Heijō palace complex to observe, record, and interpret the skies.

Reports of good or bad omens were based on readings taken from celestial and weather-related phenomena, and such omens were duly reported by the Divination Bureau to the Heavenly Sovereign. The prevailing view held that the stars and skies reacted directly to acts of good and bad governance on earth.

On the one hand, a cataclysmic natural disaster might be interpreted as an indicator of bad governance. On the other hand, if an auspicious cloud were observed in the skies then a new era name (*nengō*) might be proposed, indicating a fresh start to an auspicious new era. Astronomical observation was not about stargazing in a romanticized setting but was heavily politicized and critical to the proper functioning of the state.

83 WERE MAPS AVAILABLE?

Surviving from the Nara period are maps of the provinces, as well as maps of government-allocated rice fields indicating specific local divisions. These maps were stored at the Heijō palace complex, and most of the extant maps from this period are rice field maps.

The monk Gyōki, who lived during Shōmu's reign, is credited with drawing a map of Japan known as *Gyōkizu*. There is a Kamakura-period reproduction of *Gyōkizu* stored at a temple in Kyoto, Ninnaji.[23]

Maps relating to Heijōkyō are virtually nonexistent, although one map delineating the borders of Tōdaiji, *Tōdaiji sangai shishizu*, is an exception.

Scholars located an informal map sketched on the reverse side of an official document issued by the Office of Scripture Reproduction: gridlines on the map mark the streets of Heijōkyō and clearly indicate the location of a marketplace.

The apparent lack of Heijōkyō street maps might be due to the orderly layout of the city streets, as each street was identified by a consecutive numeral. That is, perhaps there was little need for street maps because street names were numeric grid coordinates; this naming system probably made places at Heijōkyō easy to find.

During the initial planning stage of the capital a series of detailed preparatory maps must have been drawn—but none appear to have survived.

---

23 The Kamakura period follows the Heian period, with a start date during the 1180s and ending in 1333. The political capital was moved to Kamakura, located about fifty kilometers southwest of modern-day Tokyo.

84 WAS IT POSSIBLE TO VIEW EXOTIC ANIMALS?

Visitors from foreign countries brought many kinds of animals to Heijōkyō, such as parrots, donkeys, and camels from Unified Silla.

Depictions of exotic animals have been found among the treasures stored at Shōsōin repository. Portrayed on textiles made of silk, as well as folding screens or musical instruments originating from Persia (Iran), Tang (China), and Unified Silla (Korea) are images of camels, elephants, lions, tigers, goats, parrots, and peacocks. Access to these rare objects depicting non-native animals, however, was limited to the priviledged elite.

85 AMONG THOSE WHO LIVED OUTSIDE OF HEIJŌKYŌ, HOW MUCH DID THEY KNOW ABOUT THE CITY?

There was no radio, television or internet in the eighth century, so information pertaining to the capital was not uniformly disseminated across Japan. But this does not mean that residents of other provinces knew nothing about Heijōkyō.

Each province sent conscripted workers to the capital for a term of three years, in addition to dispatching shippers who transported taxes-in-kind to Heijōkyō. Those returning home must have described life at the capital to their neighbors and friends. Traveling merchants were another source of information about the capital.

Whether intimate knowledge of the capital was widespread or not is open to speculation, but a good deal of information probably filtered through to most people living in the provinces.

PART ELEVEN:
AMUSEMENT AND FASHION

* * *

86 WHAT KINDS OF RITUAL PERFORMANCES WERE STAGED?

Singing, chanting and dance were part of nearly all rituals conducted at the Heijō palace complex and at Buddhist temples during the Nara period. For example, during the inaugural Eye Opening ceremony of the monumental Vairocana Buddha at Tōdaiji—a ceremony to ritually awaken and animate the massive icon after its completion— Buddhist scriptures were recited and a cosmopolitan array of musical accompaniments celebrated this momentous occasion. That is, the Eye Opening ceremony included performances of music and dance originating from what are now China, Korea, Vietnam, India, and Iran.

Still extant at Shōsōin repository are stylized wooden masks (*giga-kumen*) likely used to perform a kind of dramatic dance during the Eye Opening ceremony. Inscribed on the reverse side of a mask is the name of the maker and the date.

87 WHAT WERE SOME OF THE GAMES AND TOYS?

Courtiers enjoyed playing *kyokusui no utage*, a kind of outdoor drinking game. Players lined up along a stream of running water, perhaps at a garden. A cup of rice wine was slowly floated downstream and each participant had to recite a poem before the cup passed by; if successful, then the next player downstream had to recite a poem in response to the previous poem. If the cup floated by and the player did not recite a poem, the penalty was to drink the cup of wine.

Material evidence of other forms of entertainment was excavated at Heijōkyō. These include spinning tops, dice, and a toy made of wood which was shaped like a propeller on a stick that flew when spun (similar to the more familiar *taketombo* but made of wood not bamboo).

Also unearthed at Heijōkyō were white stones speculated to have been used to play *go*, a board game played with small colored stones on a board marked with gridlines. An exquisitely carved *go* board with game pieces dating to the Nara period was found inside Shōsōin repository. For some players this game was a serious affair: according to one story transcribed in a collection of oral narratives, a low-ranking government official committed murder on account of a *go* game.

Another game called *sugoroku* involved dice, and a *sugoroku* set was found inside Shōsōin repository. During the second half of the Nara period, gambling on *sugoroku* became illegal, which suggests that too many people became addicted to betting on dice.

88 DID PEOPLE PLAY SPORTS?

Courtiers engaged in sports like *uchimari* and *kemari*. *Uchimari* was relatively similar to the game of cricket, as players hit a ball with a wooden club. *Kemari* initially was a kind of military exercise, but by the Heian period evolved into a sport with several players. Participants kicked a ball, keeping it both airborne and at a certain height. A contemporary example might be Hacky Sack. There is a famous written account of two influential political figures, Prince Nakanoōe and Nakatomi Kamatari, who met while playing *kemari* under the shade of a tree (*tsukinoki*) at Asukadera during the time of the Taika Reforms in 645CE.

Sumo, a kind of Japanese wrestling, originated before the Nara period but maintained its popularity; evidence of the sport can be found among Nara-period clay vessels inscribed with characters denoting "sumo place" (*sumōsho*) and "left (side) sumo" (*hidari sumō*). Documents also inform us that Heavenly Sovereign Shōmu observed sumo matches.

Other sporting events associated with seasonal rites included a kind of race between riders on horseback (*kurabe uma*), in addition to another ritual involving the shooting of arrows by riders on horseback.

89 WERE THERE PETS?

Excavation results at the former Nagayaō residence (beneath the present Itō Yōkado Nara shopping mall) reveal many interesting details concerning pets and animals. In contrast to other Heijōkyō sites, very few remains of horses and cows were unearthed. Found instead were numerous bones of dogs, cats, deer, and mice. Aside from animal remains, also discovered were fired clay vessels with black-ink drawings of monkeys, dogs, and cranes, suggesting that these animals were kept on the property. As further evidence, excavated wooden documents refer to the custodians of horses, dogs, and cranes.

Additional wooden documents found at the site were inventory lists and receipts for animal food, informing us that dogs and cranes were fed rice, a precious commodity. Although we might like to imagine that these animals were fed valuable rice because their owners really loved them, one theory proposes that the animals were fattened up and eventually consumed by people. At any rate, the ability to feed rice to even the animals—as rice was often out of reach for the general population—reflects the immense economic power of this aristocratic household.

Elsewhere, wooden documents from the government office Kyōshiki (see Question 53) record the distribution of mice, sparrows, chickens, and horse meat to feed hawks. These raptors were kept as pets.

Cats also appear to have been pets since the Nara period, and felines imported from China were affectionately referred to as "Tang cats" (karaneko) in diaries and narratives written by aristocrats.

90 WHAT SORT OF CLOTHING DID ARISTOCRATS WEAR?

The state placed many restrictions on clothing. According to legal codes, there were two distinct categories of proper attire at the palace complex: a formal, ceremonial dress (*reifuku*) for special occasions; and a kind of uniform worn during regular working hours at government offices (*chōfuku*, *seifuku*). The color of clothing directly corresponded to a person's rank so strangers could immediately recognize who was of superior rank in an unfamiliar social setting.

The basic style of clothing probably did not change significantly from Tang Chinese styles implemented during the reign of Tenmu (r.672-686). Men wore a long-sleeved outer garment over loose-fitting white trousers or culottes (*hakama*). An ornamental belt was placed around the hips which differed according to the person's rank. Also hanging from the hips of nonmilitary government officials was a sack containing a small sword and writing implements. However, during formal ceremonies both nonmilitary and military officials carried a long sword. Each official also wore a ceremonial cap on his head, held a scepter (*shaku*), and wore shoes with white socks.

For women, the standard outfit consisted of a long-sleeved outer garment over a skirt (*mo*). The color and material of her clothing were required to be of a lower grade in relation to her spouse and father.

Surviving articles of clothing at Shōsōin repository provide many details with regard to contemporary fashions.

91 DID CLOTHING STYLES CHANGE?

Someone you know might follow the latest trends in fashion by browsing through magazines or watching movie stars. Major designers showcase new collections of clothing each season at fashion shows around the world.

For residents of Heijōkyō, the center of fashion was Tang China. Anyone who studied abroad at China and returned to Japan likely became a trendsetter who wore the most stylish clothes and became the envy of many.

Yet there were specific restrictions on the colors, materials, fabric patterns, and styles that a person was permitted to wear, so being fashionable was rather complicated. Although the government established stringent rules with regard to clothing—in order to define and maintain the status quo—it seems that many people attempted to get around the rules by incorporating new styles into their wardrobe through stealth, regardless of what was allowed.

Various written records provide a glimpse of how some people tried to circumvent the laws pertaining to clothing restrictions. Written complaints describe outrageous, illegal behavior such as using fabric of an unpermitted color on the reverse, hidden side of clothing; sewing a restricted type of fine quality material on the collar; and hanging from the cap a cord longer than what rules allow. In contemporary Japan as well, teenage students constantly push the limits of their school dress code by shortening skirt hemlines or perhaps wearing a bright red undershirt beneath a dark uniform.

A desire to creatively rearrange and circumvent strict dress codes seemingly remains unchanged.

92 WHAT DID HAIRSTYLES LOOK LIKE?

During the Tenmu reign, prior to the Nara period, new policies attempted to conform more closely to Tang Chinese practices by implementing Chinese-influenced styles of clothing, behavior at court, and general rules of decorum. For instance, the correct manner of bowing and showing deference was to kneel down and press the hands on the ground until an order was issued to prohibit this practice and replace it with a standing bow.

With regard to hairstyles, men parted their relatively long hair down the middle and bundled each side separately near the ear in a style referred to as *mizura*. Clay cylinders called *haniwa* placed atop burial mounds often represent male figures with their hair styled in this manner. However, during the late seventh century the *mizura* hairstyle was abandoned, partly to facilitate the wearing of official caps. Hair was now tightly swept up into a knot at the top of the head to fit neatly under a cap.

Official hairstyles for women changed repeatedly during this same period. During the Tenmu reign, a law stipulated that women's hair must be tied into a single ponytail at the back, a style represented in the mural paintings found inside Takamatsuzuka mounded tomb at Asukamura, Nara prefecture. Two years later, letting the hair fall loose around the shoulders was allowed as a suitable and alternative style to the single ponytail. About twenty years later, and just before the transfer of the capital from Fujiwarakyō to Heijōkyō, women were required to gather up and arrange their hair atop the head.

93 WHAT KINDS OF SHOES WERE WORN?

Courtiers participating in state ceremonies were required to wear leather shoes, and ceremonial leather shoes stored at Shōsōin repository remain extant. Military officers sometimes wore straw sandals. As for the kind of footwear worn on a daily, regular basis the archaeological record provides many clues.

Many *geta*, a kind of wooden clog, have been unearthed at Heijōkyō. Their shape resembles the *geta* still worn in Japan today—*geta* generally look like what are commonly known in English as flip flops or beach sandals but are made of wood board and cord. Also, rectangular blocks of wood secured to the underside of each wooden *geta* slightly elevate each shoe. In some *geta* retrieved during archaeological surveys, the wood surface just beneath the big toe and heel were worn down through repeated use, informing us that the shoes were used with care over a long period of time.

Also common among the general population seems to have been straw sandals or *zōri*. Only a few instances of straw sandals have been recovered, most likely because these shoes decay more readily in the ground than wooden *geta*.

Another kind of shoe was a wooden clog covering the foot, but these shoes were not commonly found and likely served as the everyday footwear for the privileged minority such as courtiers.

Wearing shoes became the norm in Japan after the Pacific War. A hot and humid place during summer months, it is unsurprising that people did not always wear shoes in Japan. Even at Heijōkyō, it seems that many people went about their daily lives in bare feet.

94 HOW DID PEOPLE ACCESSORIZE THEMSELVES?

Accessories include earrings, necklaces, bracelets, and rings. These kinds of accessories were used in Japan several thousand years before the Nara period, ever since the Jōmon period (prior to 10,000 BCE to circa 300 BCE). Personal ornaments were fashioned out of deer antlers, shells, fired clay, and translucent stones during the Jōmon period, while jewelry during subsequent periods was also made using metals and glass.

Despite this long history, widespread use of such accessories fell out of fashion during the Nara period and did not reemerge until the end of the nineteenth century during the Meiji period (1868-1912), when the state adopted European or Western cultural practices.

A limited use of accessories during the Nara period did exist as beads made of agate, amber, and crystal were strung from the hips of the Heavenly Sovereign and other high status individuals. These kinds of beads, as well as glass and rhinoceros-horn beads in the shape of a fish, were found inside Shōsōin repository, in addition to an intricately woven cord (*kumihimo*) to which the beads were attached.

Also found during excavations were a limited number of hair ornaments and combs for women that would have been inserted into a bun of hair piled atop the head. The scarcity of these objects suggests they were not used by the general population.

95 WHAT DID MOST PEOPLE WEAR?

As mentioned previously, colorful clothing made of an exquisite silk fabric and perhaps having some kind of surface design was restricted to a small, elite minority.

Low-ranking government officials were required to wear garments made of hemp that had no designs and were not dyed with any colors.

The clothing worn by the general population not employed as officials was probably quite basic and practical. *Haniwa*—clay figures placed on mounded tumuli—representing humans wore an outfit called *kantōi*, resembling a poncho and consisting of a sheet of fabric pulled down over the body with a hole for the head and often tied at the waist. Scholars believe *kantōi* was still worn during the Nara period, presumably at Heijōkyō as well.

PART TWELVE:
PRAYING AT HEIJŌKYŌ

* * *

96 WHAT WERE SOME OF THE NON-BUDDHIST PRACTICES AND BELIEFS?

During the Nara period, sickness was probably feared the most. There was no knowledge of the causes of disease, and the mysterious nature of illness probably gave rise to tremendous anxiety and fear. When someone fell ill, or if something terrible happened, the source of such misfortune was believed to emanate from a curse or other ill will directed towards that person by an enemy.

This source of evil was called *kegare* or impurities, and rituals known as *harae* sought to rid the body of *kegare*. Two distinct kinds of objects used to eliminate *kegare* are believed to have operated as a kind of substitute body. The first object, *hitogata*, was often made using wood board cut in the shape of a human body, perhaps with a face drawn in using black ink. The second object was a round clay pot resembling the shape of a human head, and a face appears in black ink on the exterior surface of the pot.

These objects were frequently unearthed from ancient riverbeds, so it seems that after a person ritually transferred their *kegare* to a *hitogata* the object was floated down a river. Likewise for the clay pot with a human face, a person probably exhaled their toxic vapors or *kegare* into the pot before placing a lid on the pot and then floating the pot down a river. This practice of cleansing the body of harmful impurities also occurred at lavish state ceremonies. *Hitogata* created out of metal are presumed to have been used by extremely high-status individuals such as the Heavenly Sovereign and royal family members.

Another non-Buddhist practice was essentially a wish for a baby to grow up strong and become successful in life—a sentiment that still echoes among parents today. Just as it remains customary in Japan to carefully save and store part of a baby's umbilical cord, families at Heijōkyō placed the placenta inside a ceramic jar, together with five copper coins, and perhaps a writing brush and ink. This jar was carefully buried by the entrance of their home, signifying a prayer for the child to grow up healthy and be blessed with a lucrative career at adulthood.

97 HOW MANY BUDDHIST TEMPLES WERE ESTABLISHED AT HEIJŌKYŌ?

The Buddhist temples at Heijōkyō generally fall into one of three categories: first, temples transferred from the old capital at Fujiwarakyō or the surrounding Asuka region to the new capital at Heijōkyō; second, temples newly established at Heijōkyō; and third, temples predating the construction of Heijōkyō that were preserved at the site.

Temples from the first category include Daianji (renamed from Daikandaiji), Yakushiji, Gangōji (renamed from Asukadera), and Kōfukuji (renamed from Umayasakadera). Since the state was involved in the construction of new temple complexes at Heijōkyō for each of these temples, they are considered to be high-ranking, great temples.

As for temples from the second category, some of the most powerful among the newly established temples include Hokkeji, Saidaiji, and Tōshōdaiji. Hokkeji was founded by Queen-consort Kōmyō and later served as the Head Nunnery of the state-sponsored, provincial temple system of nunneries (*sō kokubun niji*). The Head Monastery of the state-sponsored, provincial temple system of monasteries (*sō kokubunji*) was none other than Tōdaiji, built just outside the boundaries of Heijōkyō.

Written documents inform us that shortly after the capital was relocated to Heijōkyo, forty-eight temples were constructed. Buddhist temples in this fashion were ubiquitous at Heijōkyō. Serving as the capital for seventy-four years, it could be said that at any given time a temple was under construction somewhere inside Heijōkyō.

98 COULD ANYONE WORSHIP AT THE BUDDHIST TEMPLES?

To find out whether Buddhist temples at Heijōkyō were open to the general population, a collection of narratives and folk tales related to Buddhist phenomena, *Nihon ryōiki*, provides a few details.[24] Impoverished characters in the stories pray at the state-sponsored temples Daianji and Yakushiji, and their prayers were answered by the end of the tale. This suggests that these temples were open to the public.

Daianji and Yakushiji were established as institutions to pray for the protection, stability, and prosperity of the state, and the monks affiliated with these temples focused their energies on securing such benefits. Initially, it was illegal for monks to spread the teachings of the Buddhist law to the general populace. After a period of severe repression by government authorities, monks were eventually allowed to interact with a general lay audience and lecture on Buddhism. A particularly famous monk who was initially persecuted for his activities is Gyōki.

Tales from *Nihon ryōiki* indicate that Buddhist teachings were disseminated to Heijōkyō residents and that state temples functioned as places for the community to gather and pray.

---

24 *Nihon ryōiki* in three volumes was completed around 822 by a Yakushiji monk, Kyōkai.

PART THIRTEEN:
Relocation from Heijō to Yamashiro

* * *

99 WHY WAS THE CAPITAL TRANSFERRED TO YAMASHIRO (KYOTO)?

Heavenly Sovereign Kanmu (r. 781-806) ascended the throne at Heijōkyō. His father reigned as Heavenly Sovereign Kōnin (r. 770-781), and Kōnin was a grandson of Heavenly Sovereign Tenji. As you can see, Kōnin and Kanmu descended from the Tenji line.

Yet previous Heavenly Sovereign from the first half of the Nara period generally descended from the Tenmu line. Tenmu and Tenji are described as brothers in *Nihon shoki*. A shift in the dominant lineage started with the reign of Kōnin.

Due in part to tensions between rival lineages, Kanmu seems to have despised the Tenmu-associated Heijōkyō and, perhaps for this reason, transferred the capital further north—first to Nagaokakyō and later to Heikankyō in present-day Kyoto.

As another possible reason behind the move, Heijōkyō was filled with powerful Buddhist temples, and some scholars believe that relocating the capital was a means to break the entrenched political and economic influence of the temples and to start afresh at a new city. As supporting evidence of this view, none of the Heijōkyō temples moved to either Nagaokakyō or Heiankyō, which contrasts sharply with the earlier precedent.

A third possibility takes economic considerations into account. During the seventy-four years of the Nara period, major shifts occurred in the circulation of goods between distant provinces and the capital, which affected transportation networks and the social fabric as a whole. It may have been the case that the capital at Heijō was no longer able to sustain such activities; in order to remedy this situation and realize new methods of governance, Kanmu may have decided to transfer the capital. This line of reasoning might serve as the most appropriate interpretation for the relocation of the capital to Yamashiro (Kyoto).

100 WHAT HAPPENED TO THE SITE AT HEIJŌKYŌ AFTER IT WAS NO LONGER THE CAPITAL?

Heijōkyō served as the capital for seventy-four years, between 710 and 784, except for an interruption of approximately five years during this time. Emerging for the first time in Japan during this long period were urban city dwellers who continued to live at Heijōkyō even though the Heavenly Sovereign had moved away.

Recent excavations confirm that buildings dating back to the Nara period were still in use at Heijōkyō after the removal of the capital, and life went on as usual for a certain length of time. This is a significant point of departure from Fujiwarakyō, which served as the capital for just sixteen years and was quickly abandoned after the capital was transferred to Heijōkyō.

That the former capital at Heijō remained a viable city can be surmised from another development: Kanmu's elder son succeeded him as Heavenly Sovereign Heizei (r. 806-809), but Heizei soon abdicated in favor of his younger brother, who reigned as Heavenly Sovereign Saga (r. 809-823). Heizei left the Heian capital and returned to the Heijō palace complex, indicating that not all of the palace buildings at Heijō had been dismantled, as suitable living quarters for Heizei still remained.

In 810, shortly after Heizei abdicated, he stood in opposition to Heavenly Sovereign Saga by issuing an order to transfer the capital back to Heijōkyō. This incident is known as *Kusuko no hen* and, although Heizei was unsuccessful, this attempt highlights his continued influence and power during the Heian period, as well as the lingering significance of Heijōkyō.

Eventually, however, the former capital fell to ruin. A written account dating to 864 describes the former Heijō capital and its streets as a place buried under agricultural fields. It seems that by this time, the site where glorious Heijōkyō once stood had already reverted back, for the most part, into farming villages.

Postscript to the Japanese Edition

In 784 the capital was moved to Nagaokakyō, and Heijōkyō ceased to function as a government center. Although Heijōkyō reverted to agricultural farmland, the grid street layout still served to demarcate land divisions and streets. If you look closely at a modern map of Nara city, you might be able to envision a faint image of the former capital. Now that you have read the 100 Questions & Answers provided in this book, we hope you were able to get acquainted with Heijōkyō.

When preparations were being made by Nara prefecture to commemorate the 1300th anniversary year of Heijōkyō in 2010, those of us who excavate the ruins of Heijōkyō at the public institution, Archaeological Institute of Kashihara, Nara Prefecture, thought about how to contribute to the body of knowledge concerning Heijōkyō. That was the starting point for this book.

As for how we selected the hundred questions, we were assisted by a teacher at Shinsei Shōyō Senior High School (Nara kenritsu Shinsei Shōyō kōkō), Kano Tomomichi, who was receiving special training at the Museum affiliated with Archaeological Institute of Kashihara. Some of his questions baffled us, and we struggled to find appropriate responses. In so doing, our own ignorance and lack of understanding with regard to basic questions became evident, and this project served as a critical learning experience for us all.

Responses to the hundred questions were researched and written by six people, starting with the general director, Sugaya Fuminori, followed by Hayashibe Hitoshi, Tsurumi Yasutoshi, Shigemi Yasushi, Suzuki Kazuyoshi, and Satō Asako. Satō also provided illustrations and drawings in the Japanese edition. Although we consulted many books, we hope you will forgive us for listing the references in a bibliography compiled at the end of the Japanese edition instead of providing notes to each reference.

Still to come are more excavations at Heijōkyō. Some of our responses may eventually become discredited or disproved on the basis of new discoveries, or perhaps new questions will emerge. The study of Heijōkyō is anything but finished, so please look forward to learning about surprising new finds during forthcoming excavations.

During the preparation of this book, Tateishi Kenji of the Association for Commemorative Events of the 1300th Anniversary of Nara Heijōkyō Capital (Heijō sento sensanbyakunen jigyō kyōkai) offered much appreciated advice and guidance. We are also grateful to the various institutions who gave us permission to publish reproductions of their images. We extend our appreciation to the president of the publishing company for the Japanese edition of the book, Tsuruoka Ichirō at Gakuseisha and the managing editor, Kodama Yūhei.

Finally, we thank all of our readers who provided the inspiration for this book.

Sugaya Fuminori
General director
Archaeological Institute of Kashihara, Nara Prefecture
(October 2010)

Glossary

Akishino 秋篠 (Q57) (name of a river)

aoi アオイ (Q43) Malvaceae

Arima 有馬 (Q33) (name of a location)

Asukadera 飛鳥寺 (Q88) (name of a Buddhist temple)

Asukamura 明日香村 (Q25) Asuka Village

Ayame ike 菖蒲池 (Q50) (name of a train station)

biwa 琵琶 (Q15) lute

bō 坊 ward; column; the area between two column avenues

bō ōji 坊大路 column avenue; north-south avenue

Chang'an 長安 (Q4) ancient capital in Tang China

chi 笞 (Q28) beating the buttocks with a bamboo cane as punishment

chisha チシャ (Q43) lettuce

chō 調 (Q65) taxes in the form of food and craft products

chōfuku 朝服 (Q90) court attire for officials with rank

chōga 朝賀 (Q13) a state ceremony held on first day of new year

Chōshūden 朝集殿 (Q55) State Assembly Halls

Chōdō 朝堂 State Hall

chūgi 籌木 (Q31) flat wood strips functioning like toilet paper

Chūsenshi 鋳銭司 (Q67) Office of Minting Coins

Daianji 大安寺 (Q6) (name of a Buddhist temple)

Daibutsuden 大仏殿 (Q54) Great Buddha Hall at Tōdaiji

daidairon 大大論 (Q30) "big big discussion"

Daigakuryō 大学寮 (Q78) Bureau of Higher Education, Court University

Daigokuden 大極殿 Great Audience Hall

Daikandaiji 大官大寺 (Q97) (name of a Buddhist temple)

Daikoku no shiba 大黒の芝 "Daikoku['s] grass"

dainagon 大納言(Q1) senior counselor

Dairi 内裏 (Q9) Inner (Residential) Palace

Daijōkan 太政官 (Q73) Council of State

Dōgo 道後 (Q33) (name of a location)

eji 衛士 (Q16) palace guards

Engishiki 延喜式 (Q63) (name of an ancient text)

Fujiwara Fuhito 藤原不比等 (Q1) (name of a historical figure)

Fujiwarakyō 藤原京 (Q10) Fujiwara capital

Fujiwarakyū 藤原宮 Fujiwara palace

Fukisaki 房前 (Q73) (name of a historical figure)

fukuoku 副屋 (Q23) secondary building

fūtaku 風鐸 (Q54) wind bell

Gangōji 元興寺 (Q8) (name of a Buddhist temple)

Ganjin (Ch. Jianzhen) 鑑真 (Q55) (name of a historical figure)

Gakuseisha 学生社 (name of a publisher)

Gekyō 外京 (Q8) Outer Capital

Genbō 玄昉 (Q64) (name of a historical figure)

genkan 阮咸 (Q15) lute with a flat body

genmai 玄米 (Q41) unpolished rice

Genmei tennō 元明天皇 (name of a Heavenly Sovereign)

Genshiryō 関市令 (Q69) (name of a set of laws)

geta 下駄 (Q93) wooden clogs

gigakumen 伎楽面 (Q86) mask used to perform ancient dramatic dance

gishi gishi ギシギシ (Q43) a kind of buckwheat; curly dock

gisō 義倉 (Q36) granary used to store emergency food supplies

go 碁 (Q87) Go game

Gojō 五条 (Q8) Fifth Street

Gokoku hōjō 五穀豊穣 (Q38) bountiful harvest (of the five sacred grains)

Gokuryō 獄令 (Q28) (name of a set of laws)

guchūreki 具注暦 (Q26) a kind of calendar

Gyōki 行基 (Q37) (name of a historical figure)

Gyōkizu 行基図 (Q83) (name of a map of Japan)

Hachigyaku 八虐 (Q27) the eight felonies under the ritsuryō system

hajiki 土師器 (Q46) low-fired earthenware

hakama 袴 (Q90) trousers

haniwa 埴輪 (Q6) ceramic funerary sculpture placed on mounded tomb surface

harae 祓え (Q96) purification rituals

Harima 播磨 (Q66) (name of an ancient province)

Hashi 波斯 (Q62) Persia

Hayashibe Hitoshi 林部均 (name of an author of the Japanese edition of this book)

Heijōkyō 平城京 Nara capital

Heijōkyō sakyō gojō shibō 平城京左京五条四坊 (Q66) East Fourth Ward, Fifth Street

Heijōkyō sakyō hachijō sanbō 平城京左京八条三坊 (Q57) East Third Ward, Eighth Street

Heijōkyō sakyō sanjō nibō 平城京左京三条二坊 (Q56) East Second Ward, Third Street

Heijōkyō ukyō hachijō nibō 平城京右京八条二坊 (Q57) West Second Ward, Eighth Street

Heijōkyū 平城宮 Nara palace

Heijō sento sensanbyakunen jigyō kyōkai 平城遷都一三〇〇年事業協会 Association for Commemorative Events of the 1300th Anniversary of Nara Heijōkyō Capital

Heiwadai kyūjō 平和台球場 (Q60) Heiwadai stadium

Heizei 平城 (Q100) (name of a Heavenly Sovereign)

hidari sumō 左相撲 (Q88) "left sumo"

Hieda iseki 稗田遺跡 (Q37) Hieda site

Higashi horikawa 東堀川 (Q57) East Canal

Higashi kujō chō 東九条町 (Q57) (name of a district within Nara city)

Higashi no ichi 東の市 (Q57) East Marketplace

hitogata 人形 (Q96) human-shaped effigy

Hokkeji 法華寺 (Q33) (name of a Buddhist temple)

Hokurikudō 北陸道 (Q35) (name of an ancient circuit and region)

Honsō 本草 (Q74) (name of an ancient text)

Hōraisan kofun 宝来山古墳 (Q6) (name of a mounded tomb)

hottate bashira 掘立柱 (Q23) embedded-pillar building

hyōe 兵衛 (Q16) military guard

Ichiba kofun 市庭古墳 (Q6) (name of a mounded tomb)

ichibito 市人 (Q17) merchant at the marketplace

Ichijō kōkō 一条高校 (Q80) Ichijō High School

Ichi no tsukasa 市司 (Q68) Office of the Markets

go 碁 (Q87) Go game

Ikomayama 生駒山 (Q37) Mount Ikoma

Ishigami iseki 石神遺跡 (Q26) Ishigami site

Ishitsuryō 医疾令 (Q74) (name of a set of laws)

Isonokami Maro 石上麻呂 (Q1) (name of a historical figure)

Isonokami Yakatsugu 石上宅嗣 (Q80) (name of a historical figure)

itabuki 板葺 (Q23) wood board roof

itto 一斗 (Q67) a unit of cubic measure; equivalent to 18.039 liters

Izumi 和泉 (Q16) (name of an ancient province)

Jingō kaihō 神功開宝 (Q67) (name of a coin)

jō 杖 (Q28) beating the buttocks with a rod in punishment

jō 条 row; street; the area between two rows of streets

jō ōji 条大路 (Q56) row avenue; east-west avenue

jōbō 条坊 (Q50) city street plan organized on a rectangular grid

jōrisei 条里制 (Q11) agricultural reallocation under the ritsuryō system, using approximately one-hectare squares as the main grid unit

Kaiki shōhō 開基勝宝 (Q67) (name of a gold coin)

kami 神 (Q74) deity

Kanmu 桓武 (Q99) (name of a Heavenly Sovereign)

Kano Tomomichi 鹿野智道 (name of a contributor to the Japanese edition of this book)

kanshi 干支 (Q26) the sexagenary cycle

kanshoku 間食 (Q48) to eat between regular mealtimes

kantōi 貫頭衣 (Q95) tunic made from a single piece of cloth

Karamomo chō 杏町 (Q57) (name of a district within Nara city)

karaneko 唐猫 (Q89) a Chinese cat

kasuyuzake 糟湯酒 (Q49) a hot beverage made using the lees from rice wine

katashiro 形代 (Q70) effigy used in purification rites as a substitute for a deity or person

Kawachi 河内 (Q16) (name of an ancient province)

kayabuki 茅葺 (Q23) thatch roof

kayakin 伽耶琴 (Q15) gayageum; a traditional Korean zither-like stringed instrument

kegare 汚れ (Q70) pollution; impurities

keichō 計帳 (Q19) population registry

kemari 蹴鞠 (Q88) a kind of ball game

kentōshi 遣唐使 (Q49) Japanese envoy to Tang China

Kibi Makibi 吉備真備 (Q64) (name of a historical figure)

kin 琴 (Q15) Japanese zither

Kinai 畿内 (Q16) (name of a specific group of ancient provinces)

kinako きな粉 (Q44) soybean flour

kitaguchi 北口 (Q50) north exit

Kitaura Sadamasa 北浦定政 (name of an early modern figure)

Kodama Yūhei 児玉有平 (name of the editor at Gakuseisha)

Kōfukuji 興福寺 (Q8) (name of a Buddhist temple)

kofun 古墳 (Q6) tumulus (mounded tomb)

kōji 麹 (Q49) yeast; mold; malt

Kojiki 古事記 (Q37) (name of an ancient text)

Kokoku 胡国 (Q62) (name of an ancient state in northern China)

kokugunri 国郡里 (Q5) province, county, administrative village

kōkyo 皇居 (Q12) the current Imperial Palace, now located at Tokyo

Kōmyō 光明 (name of a Queen-consort)

Kōnin 光仁 (Q99) (name of a Heavenly Sovereign)

Konron 崑崙 (Q62) (name of an ancient state)

Kōriyama 郡山 (Q50) (name of a train station)

Kōrokan 鴻臚館 (Q60) Foreign Envoys' Quarters

koseki 戸籍 (Q14) census or family registers

kubunden 口分田 (Q18) rice fields allotted to individual subjects from which yields were taxed by the government

kugo 箜篌 (Q15) harp

Kujō chō 九条町 (Q57) (name of a district in Nara city)

Kūkai 空海 (Q64) (name of a historical figure)

kumihimo 組み紐 (Q94) braided string

kurabe uma くらべ馬 (Q88) horse-racing

kuretsuzumi 腰鼓 (Q15) hand drum

Kusuko no hen 薬子の変 (Q100) (name of a political disturbance)

Kyōbate 京終 (Q50) (name of a train station)

Kyōkai 景戒 (Q98) (name of a historical figure)

kyōko 京戸 (Q18) resident of the capital

kyokusui no utage 曲水の宴 (Q87) a kind of drinking game

Kyōshiki 京職 (Q53) an administrative office governing a sector of the capital

Kyūshū nanbu 九州南部 (Q22) southern Kyūshū

manbyō kō 万病膏 (Q74) "remedy for all (literally, ten-thousand) kinds of disease"

Mannen tsūhō 万年通宝 (Q67) (name of a coin)

Man'yōshū 万葉集 (Q12) (name of an ancient text)

Maro 麻呂 (Q73) (name of a historical figure)

Mikinotsukasa 造酒司 (Q49) Office of Rice-wine Production

miya 宮 (Q12) palace

Mizuochi iseki 水落遺跡 (Q25) Mizouchi site

mizura 美豆良 (Q92) styling one's hair into a bun on each side of the head

mo 裳 (Q90) long skirt

Moitori no tsukasa 主水司 (Q67) Office of Water, Rice Porridge, and Ice

mokkan 木簡 (Q5) wooden writing tablet

mon 文 (Q67) a unit of currency

Monmu 文武 (Q33) (name of a Heavenly Sovereign)

Muchimaro 武智麻呂 (Q73) (name of a historical figure)

Nagaokakyō 長岡京 (Q55) Nagaoka capital

Nagayaō 長屋王 (Q17) Prince Nagaya

Nahoyama 奈保山 (Q37) Naho Hill

Nakanoōe 中大兄 (Q25) (name of a prince)

Nakatomi (Fujiwara) Kamatari 中臣(藤原)鎌足 (Q88) (name of a historical figure)

Nakatsukasashō 中務省 (Q80) Ministry of Central Affairs

Naniwa no tsu 難波津 (Q60) official port of Naniwa

Nankaidō 南海道 (Q35) (name of an ancient circuit and region)

Nara (in Man'yōshū) 楢 or 奈良 (Q12) Nara

Nara kenritsu Kashihara kōkogaku kenkyūjo 奈良県立橿原考古学研究所 Archaeological Institute of Kashihara, Nara prefecture

Nara kenritsu Shinsei Shōyō kōkō 奈良県立榛生昇陽高校 Nara Prefectural Shinseishōyō Senior High School

Naramachi ならまち (Q50) (name of a district in Nara city)

Nara no miyako 寧楽の京師 (Q12) capital at Nara

Narashi kyōiku iinkai 奈良市教育委員会 (Q54) Nara-city Board of Education

narezushi 熟鮨 (Q42) a kind of sushi made using fermented fish

Nihonkoku kenzaisho mokuroku 日本国見在書目録 (Q80) (name of an ancient text)

Nihon ryōiki 日本霊異記 (Q98) (name of an ancient text)

Nenbutsujiyama kofun 念仏寺山古墳 (Q6) (name of a mounded tomb)

nengō 年号 (Q82) the era name

nigori sake 濁り酒 (Q49) unfiltered rice wine

Nihon shoki 日本書紀 (Q33) (name of an ancient text)

Nijō 二条 (Q8) Second Street

niko 二鼓 (Q15) a drum

Ninnaji 仁和寺 (Q83) (name of a Buddhist temple)

Nishi horikawa 西堀川 (Q57) West Canal

Nishi no ichi 西の市 (Q57) West Marketplace

nobiru ノビル (Q43) Allium macrostemon; wild rocambole

nuhi 奴婢 (Q16) slave

ōharae 大祓 (Q27) Great Purification Ceremony

Onmyōryō 陰陽寮 (Q24) Divination Bureau

Ono Oyu 小野老 (Q51) (name of a historical figure)

Ōno ri 大野里 (Q5) Ōno administrative village

osa 訳語 (Q22) translator; interpreter

Ōtomo Tabito 大伴旅人 (Q51) (name of a historical figure)

Ōtomo Yakamochi 大伴家持 (Q52) (name of a historical figure)

Ōtomo Yotsuna 大伴四綱 (Q51) (name of a historical figure)

Ō Yasumaro 太安萬侶 (Q37) (name of a historical figure)

Parhae 渤海 (Q13) Bohai; an ancient Korean kingdom

raden shitan gogen biwa 螺鈿紫檀五絃琵琶 (Q15) a red sandalwood five-stringed lute with inlay

rajō 羅城 (Q29) city walls

Rajōmon 羅城門 (Q29) Rajō Gate; main gate to the capital

reifuku 礼服 (Q90) ceremonial court attire

Rinyū 林邑 (Q59) Vietnam

rōkoku hakase 漏刻博士 (Q24) government specialist who read the time on the water clock

Rongo (Ch. Lunyu) 論語 (Q79) (name of an ancient text)

ru 流(Q28) banishment as a form of punishment

sadaijin 左大臣 (Q1) Minister of the Left

Saeki Imaemishi 佐伯今毛人 (Q64) (name of a historical figure)

Saga 嵯峨 (Q100) (name of a Heavenly Sovereign)

Sagami 相模 (Q66) (name of an ancient province)

Sahoyama 佐保山 (Q37) Saho Hill

Saichō 最澄 (Q64) (name of a historical figure)

Saidaiji 西大寺 (Q5) (name of a Buddhist temple)

Saikaidō 西海道 (Q35) (name of an ancient circuit and region)

sake kasu 酒粕 (Q49) rice wine lees

Sakyō 左京 (Q8) Left Capital

San'indō 山陰道 (Q35) (name of an ancient circuit and region)

Sanjō ōji 三条大路 (Q56) Third Street

Sanshō サンショウ (Q45) Zanthoxylum; prickly ash

Sanyōdō 山陽道 (Q35) (name of an ancient circuit and region)

Satō Asako 佐藤麻子 (name of an author of the Japanese edition of this book)

Sawada Goichi 澤田吾一 (Q18) (name of a modern scholar)

sechie 節会 (Q13) royal banquet held during special seasonal holidays

seifuku 制服 (Q90) court attire for officials with no rank

seishu 清酒 (Q49) filtered rice wine

Sekino Tadashi 関野貞(name of a modern scholar)

senbei せんべい (Q44) a cracker-like snack

Senjimon (Ch. Qianziwen) 千字文 (Q79) (name of an ancient text)

senmyō 宣命 (Q12) a royal proclamation

sento 遷都 relocation of the capital

setsujitsu 節日(Q13) holiday celebrating seasonal change

settō 筋刀 (Q64) ceremonial sword

Settsu 摂津 (Q16) (name of an ancient province)

Seyakuin 施薬院 (Q74) (name of a medical dispensary, established as a subtemple of Kōfukuji)

shaku 笏 (Q90) scepter

shakuhachi 尺八 (Q15) flute

Shakyōsho 写経所 (Q33) Office of Scripture Reproduction

shi 死 (Q28) death as a form of punishment

shichō 仕丁 (Q53) maintenance crew for street gutters

Shigemi Yasushi 重見泰 (name of an author of the Japanese edition of this book)

shii シイ (Q44) Castanopsis

Shikibushō 式部省 (Q78) Ministry of Civil Services and Ceremonies

Shikoku 四国 (Q35) (name of a region)

Shimeno kofun 神明野古墳 (Q6) (name of a mounded tomb)

Shimotsu michi 下ツ道 (Q5) (name of an ancient road)

shiragigoto 新羅琴 (Q15) a zither

Shirahama 白浜 (Q33) (name of a location)

Shirai Hsueh Yoko 白井薛陽子 (name of the book translator)

shishin 四神 (Q3) the Four (Daoist) Divinities

shōchū 焼酎 (Q49) Japanese spirits distilled from sweet potatoes and other ingredients

Shōdaiji konryū engi 招提寺建立縁起 (Q55) (name of an ancient text)

Shoku nihongi 続日本紀 (Q12) (name of an ancient text)

Shōmu 聖武 (name of a Heavenly Sovereign)

Shōrin'en 松林苑 (Q56) (name of an ancient garden)

Shōsōin 正倉院 Shōsōin Treasure Repository

shuoku 主屋 (Q23) primary or main building

shushi 酒肆 (Q49) an ancient drinking establishment

Silla 新羅 (Q13) (name of an ancient Korean kingdom)

so 祖 (Q65) agricultural produce tax

sō 筝 (Q15) a long zither

Soejimo 添下 (Q5) (name of an ancient county predating the Nara capital)

Soekami 添上 (Q5) (name of an ancient county predating the Nara capital)

sō kokubunji (総)国分寺 (Q97) (the head of the) provincial monastery system

sō kokubun niji (総)国分尼寺 (Q97) (the head of the) provincial nunnery system

sueki 須恵器 (Q46) unglazed stoneware

Sugawara 菅原 (Q5) (name of a location)

Sugaya Fuminori 菅谷文則 (name of an author of the Japanese edition of this book)

Sugiyama kofun 杉山古墳 (Q6) (name of a mounded tomb)

sugoroku 双六 (Q87) dice game

sumōsho 相撲所 (Q88) "sumo place"

Suzaku 朱雀 (Q4) (name of the main north-south boulevard to the palace complex)

Suzuki Kazuyoshi 鈴木一議 (name of an author of the Japanese edition of this book)

Taihei genpō 太平元宝 (Q67) (name of silver coin)

Taihō ritsuryō 大宝律令 (Q28) Taihō penal and administrative code

taishi 大使 (Q64) Great Envoy

Takamatsuzuka 高松塚 (Q92) (name of a mounded tomb)

Tanada Kajūrō 棚田嘉十郎 (name of an early modern preservationist)

tara no me タラの芽 (Q43) Aralia elata

taketombo 竹トンボ (Q87) a spinning toy made of bamboo

Tateishi Kenji 立石堅志 (name of a contributor to the Japanese edition of this book)

tatemae たてまえ (Q29) theory

Tegaimon 転害門 (Q50) Tegai Gate

Tenji 天智 (Q25) (name of a Heavenly Sovereign)

Tenjiku 天竺 (Q59) India

Tenmu 天武 (Q90) (name of a Heavenly Sovereign)

tennō 天皇 Heavenly Sovereign

Tenpyō 天平 (name of an era)

Tenyakuryō 典薬寮 (Q74) Bureau of Medicine

Tōdaiji 東大寺 (name of a Buddhist temple)

Tōdaiji sangai shishizu 東大寺山堺四至図 (Q83) (name of an ancient map)

Tōdaiji yōroku 東大寺要録 (Q54) (name of an ancient text)

Tōdō 藤堂 (name of a feudal domain in what is now Mie prefecture)

Tōhoku chihō 東北地方 (Q22) (name of a region)

Tōin 東院 (Q56) East Palace

Tōin teien 東院庭園 (Q56) East Palace Garden

Tōkaidō 東海道 (Q35) (name of an ancient circuit and region)

toraijin 渡来人 (Q78) people who crossed the seas; immigrants to Japan

Tōsandō 東山道 (Q35) (name of an ancient circuit and region)

Tōshōdaiji 唐招提寺 (Q55) (name of a Buddhist temple)

tsukinoki 槻樹 (Q88) Japanese Zelkova

Tsukushi no murotsumi 筑紫館 (Q60) Foreign Envoys' Quarters in Tsukushi province

Tsurumi Yasutoshi 鶴見泰寿 (name of an author of the Japanese edition of this book)

Tsuruoka Ichirō 鶴岡一郎 (name of the President of Gakuseisha)

uchimari 打毬 (Q88) a kind of ball game

udaijin 右大臣 (Q1) Minister of the Right

Ukyō 右京 (Q8) Right Capital

Umakai 宇合 (Q73) (name of a historical figure)

umaya 駅家 (Q35) official post station along the ancient circuits where horses were stabled

Umayasakadera 厩坂寺 (Q97) (name of a Buddhist temple)

unkyakufu 運脚夫 (Q66) a shipper

Untei 芸亭 (Q80) name of first library in Japan

Usa Hachiman 宇佐八幡 (Q28) (name of a shrine)

Wadō kaichin 和同開珎 (Q67) (name of a coin)

"Wadō kaihō" 和銅開寶 (Q67) (name of a coin)

wagon 和琴 (Q15) a zither

Waké Kiyomaro 和気清麻呂 (Q28) (name of a historical figure)

Wakébe Kitanamaro 別部穢麿 (Q28) (name of a historical figure)

warabi ワラビ (Q43) Allium macrostemon; Japanese bracken

Yakushiji 薬師寺 (Q97) (name of a Buddhist temple)

yamaimo ヤマイモ (Q43) Dioscorea japonica; yam

Yamanoue Okura 山上憶良 (Q64) (name of a historical figure)

Yamashiro 山城 or 山背 (Q16) (name of an ancient province)

Yamato 大和 (Q16) (name of an ancient province)

Yamato Kōriyama 大和郡山 (Q37) (name of a city)

yō 庸 (Q65) labour tax

yokobue 横笛 (Q15) horizontally blown flute

yukatabira 湯帳 (Q33) a kind of garment worn while bathing

yuya 湯屋 (Q33) bath

zōri 草履 (Q93) traditional sandals woven from dried grasses

zōyō 雑徭 (Q65) additional labour tax

zu 徒 (Q28) imprisonment as a form of punishment

Zushoryō 図書寮 (Q80) Bureau of Books and Drawings

www.ingramcontent.com/pod-product-compliance
Lightning Source LLC
Chambersburg PA
CBHW071357310526
45789CB00020B/390